CryptoCraft

**Cryptocurrency Market Dynamics:
Analyzing Trends for Optimal Trading Outcomes**

Sophia Grayson

Table of Contents

INTRODUCTION

Welcome to "CryptoCraft: Cryptocurrency Market Dynamics - Analyzing Trends for Optimal Trading Outcomes." Cryptocurrencies have become a groundbreaking financial phenomenon in a society increasingly embracing digital innovations. Cryptocurrencies have caught the attention of both traders and investors because of their potential for high returns, decentralized nature, and technological underpinnings.

More than just luck is needed to navigate the complicated world of cryptocurrency trading successfully; you also need a thorough understanding of market dynamics, trends, and the variables affecting price changes. This book is your in-depth guide for mastering the art of cryptocurrency trading through a careful examination of current market conditions. You'll be able to make decisions that can result in the best trading outcomes by exploring the complexities of technical, fundamental, and sentiment analysis.

Although there is undeniable potential for substantial profits in the cryptocurrency market, there is also undeniable risk involved. Because of the volatility of cryptocurrencies, traders may find themselves subject to erratic market swings if they lack a firm understanding of the underlying dynamics. This book strives to close the gap between inexperienced investors and traders by giving you practical advice based on research and strategy.

We'll take you on an exploration of the cryptocurrency trading industry in the following chapters. Initially, we'll lay a solid foundation by exposing you to the fundamental ideas of cryptocurrencies, blockchain technology, and the function of exchanges. After that, we'll explore the fundamentals of trading while delving into technical and fundamental analysis nuances. We'll show you how sentiment analysis works and how it affects market movements, giving you the skills necessary to sort through the noise in news and social media.

After a solid grasp of analysis methods, we'll focus on identifying and deciphering market trends and patterns. With this information, you'll be better equipped to create trading plans that meet your objectives and risk tolerance. We'll talk about different trading approaches and get into risk-management strategies essential for protecting your capital in this volatile market.

But knowledge alone isn't enough; you need a plan. Due to this, we will walk you through the process of creating a trading plan specific to your skills and goals. We'll conclude with case studies from real-world transactions to draw out practical insights.

This book is created to give you insights, strategies, and a comprehensive approach to navigating the cryptocurrency market, whether you're a beginner eager to understand the nuances of cryptocurrency trading or an experienced trader trying to improve your strategy. Prepare to delve into the depths of market dynamics, examine patterns, and make judgments with confidence that can produce the best trading results.

Let's take this journey and realize the possibilities of trading cryptocurrencies!

CHAPTER I

Understanding Cryptocurrency Markets

Definition of cryptocurrency

In the vast landscape of modern finance, cryptocurrency stands as a transformative force, redefining the very concept of value in the digital age. Cryptocurrency is fundamentally a virtual or digital currency that uses cryptography to guarantee the security of transactions and regulates the production of new units. This revolutionary form of currency operates on decentralized systems, utilizing blockchain technology to ensure transparency, immutability, and security.

The cornerstone of any cryptocurrency is its decentralized nature. Unlike traditional fiat currencies issued and regulated by central banks, cryptocurrencies operate on decentralized networks built upon blockchain technology. A distributed, tamper-resistant digital ledger called a blockchain keeps track of all transactions made by means of a network of computers. Because of this decentralization, there is no longer a need for intermediaries like banks to validate and verify transactions.

Bitcoin, introduced in 2009 by the pseudonymous creator Satoshi Nakamoto, is hailed as the pioneering cryptocurrency. Its creation marked a paradigm shift in how we perceive and interact with money. Bitcoin's underlying technology, the blockchain, serves as a public and transparent ledger detailing every transaction made with the currency. This transparent ledger has fundamentally altered how trust is established and maintained in financial transactions, fostering a new level of accountability.

The creation and management of cryptocurrencies are intricately tied to complex cryptographic algorithms. Mining, a term commonly associated with cryptocurrency, refers to the process by which new cryptocurrency units are generated and added to the blockchain. Miners use powerful computers to solve intricate mathematical puzzles, with the first to solve the puzzle adding a new block to the blockchain and acquiring a reward in cryptocurrency. This process not only ensures the network's security but also controls the issuance of new units, safeguarding against inflation.

Furthermore, the cryptographic nature of cryptocurrencies ensures the security and privacy of transactions. Every transaction is secured with cryptographic keys: a public key, which serves as an address to receive funds, and a private key, which is used to access and control those funds. This encryption ensures that transactions are secure, transparent, and traceable without revealing sensitive personal information.

Cryptocurrencies transcend geographical borders and are accessible to anyone with an internet connection. This global accessibility can empower individuals lacking access to traditional banking services, enabling them to participate in financial transactions and investments. Additionally, cryptocurrencies facilitate cross-border transactions, eliminating the need for costly intermediaries and reducing the time it takes for funds to be transferred internationally.

However, the world of cryptocurrencies has its challenges. Concerns have been raised about the volatility of cryptocurrency prices, which can occasionally undergo dramatic swings over very short time periods. As governments struggle with how to handle the unique challenges presented by decentralized currencies that transcend their jurisdictional control, regulatory considerations also loom large.

In conclusion, the definition of cryptocurrency extends beyond its digital nature; it embodies a paradigm shift in how we perceive, store, and exchange value. Rooted in the principles of decentralization, cryptography, and transparency, cryptocurrencies offer a glimpse into a future where financial systems are more inclusive, secure, and efficient. As this technology evolves, its impact on the world of finance and beyond is poised to be revolutionary.

Overview of the blockchain technology

In the ever-evolving landscape of technology, few innovations have garnered as much attention and potential as blockchain. Emerging as the underlying framework for cryptocurrencies, blockchain technology has transcended its initial application to revolutionize industries far beyond finance. At its core, blockchain is a decentralized and tamper-resistant digital ledger that records transactions across a network of computers. This section delves into the intricacies of blockchain technology, exploring its architecture, benefits, challenges, and profound impact on various sectors.

The foundation of blockchain technology lies in its decentralized nature. A blockchain runs on a distributed network of nodes, as opposed to conventional centralized systems, where data is maintained and controlled by a single institution. Because each node has a copy of the full blockchain, redundancy is maintained and a single point of failure is avoided. This decentralized architecture enhances security and resiliency, as no single point is vulnerable to hacking or manipulation.

At the heart of a blockchain is its structure of blocks, each containing a batch of transactions. These blocks are linked in a chronological sequence, forming an immutable chain. Without the agreement of the majority of the network, a block that was previously added to the blockchain cannot be altered or deleted. This immutability, combined with cryptographic hashing, ensures the integrity of the data stored within the blockchain.

Transparency is one of the main advantages of blockchain technology. In a public blockchain, every transaction is visible to all participants on the network. This transparency fosters trust and accountability, as any attempt to alter past transactions would also require changing subsequent blocks, a task virtually impossible due to the computational power required. This characteristic has profound implications for industries like supply chain management, where the entire journey of a product can be traced and verified in real-time.

Another hallmark feature of blockchain is its security. Transaction security and blockchain access control are both achieved through the use of cryptography. Participants are assigned cryptographic keys: a public key, which acts as an address for receiving transactions, and a private key, which provides access to initiate transactions. This encryption ensures that transactions are secure and authenticated, mitigating the risk of unauthorized access and fraud.

Smart contracts, executable code that automatically enforces predefined rules when certain conditions are met, represent a further evolution of blockchain technology. These self-executing contracts streamline complicated procedures, eliminating the requirement for middlemen and lowering the risk of mistakes. They find applications in various fields, from legal agreements to real estate transactions, streamlining processes and enhancing efficiency.

While blockchain technology holds immense promise, it also faces challenges that must be addressed. Scalability is one such challenge, as traditional blockchains like Bitcoin and Ethereum have encountered limitations in processing a high volume of transactions simultaneously. Solutions like sharding and layer-2 protocols are being explored to enhance scalability without compromising security.

Energy consumption is another area of concern, particularly for proof-of-work blockchains. The computational power required for mining and adding new blocks to the blockchain has raised questions about the environmental impact. Some projects are shifting to more energy-efficient consensus mechanisms like proof-of-stake, where validators are chosen based on the amount of cryptocurrency they hold.

Beyond cryptocurrencies, blockchain technology has enormous potential. Industries such as healthcare, supply chain, finance, and even governance are exploring its application to enhance transparency, security, and efficiency. In healthcare, patient data can be securely stored and shared while ensuring privacy and consent.

Supply chains can be revolutionized by tracking the origin and journey of goods, reducing counterfeiting and providing ethical sourcing. Decentralized finance (DeFi) is reshaping the financial landscape by offering services like lending, borrowing, and trading without intermediaries. In

conclusion, the overview of blockchain technology reveals a paradigm shift in how data is managed, secured, and shared. Its decentralized and transparent nature has the potential to reshape industries and empower individuals by placing control back into their hands. While challenges exist, ongoing research and innovation are addressing these issues, unlocking the full potential of this transformative technology. As blockchain continues to evolve, its impact on the digital world and beyond promises to be profound and enduring.

Types of cryptocurrencies and their significance

In the dynamic realm of cryptocurrencies, diversity is a defining characteristic. Beyond the ubiquity of Bitcoin, the pioneer cryptocurrency, many alternative digital currencies have emerged, each with its unique features, purposes, and underlying technologies. This section explores the various types of cryptocurrencies and delves into their significance in shaping the digital economy, offering a glimpse into the multifaceted landscape of decentralized finance.

Bitcoin, often referred to as digital gold, holds the distinction of being the first cryptocurrency. Conceived by the enigmatic Satoshi Nakamoto, Bitcoin introduced the concept of a decentralized digital currency, free from the control of central banks or governments. Its primary use case initially revolved around peer-to-peer transactions and an alternative store of value. Over time, Bitcoin's significance has evolved, solidifying its position as a hedge against inflation and a sought-after asset for investment diversification.

The term "altcoin" collectively refers to all cryptocurrencies other than Bitcoin. This diverse category encompasses various digital currencies, each with its unique focus and technological innovation. For instance, Ethereum pioneered the idea of smart contracts, paving the way for the development of decentralized autonomous organizations (DAOs) and decentralized applications (DApps). This innovation propelled the growth of the decentralized finance (DeFi) ecosystem, reimagining traditional financial services without intermediaries.

Privacy coins, like Monero and Zcash, address a critical concern in the cryptocurrency space: transaction privacy. Unlike Bitcoin, where transactions are transparent and traceable on the blockchain, privacy coins employ advanced cryptographic techniques to obscure transaction details, offering enhanced privacy and confidentiality. While their significance is undeniable in safeguarding financial privacy, these coins have also raised concerns about potential misuse for illicit activities.

Amid the volatile price swings of many cryptocurrencies, stablecoins have emerged as a solution to maintain price stability. These digital assets are typically pegged to stable assets like fiat currencies or commodities, ensuring their value remains relatively constant. The significance of stablecoins lies in their role as a bridge between the traditional financial world and the cryptocurrency ecosystem. They facilitate quick and low-cost transfers, acting as a hedge during market downturns and a means for traders to exit positions swiftly.

Utility tokens are intrinsic to specific blockchain platforms or applications, serving a practical purpose within their respective ecosystems. They provide access to network features, services, or products. The significance of utility tokens extends beyond mere transactions; they fuel interactions within decentralized applications, incentivizing participation, and enabling ecosystem growth. Examples include Chainlink (LINK), which powers decentralized oracle networks, and Binance Coin (BNB), which is used to pay charges for trading on the Binance exchange.

Security tokens represent ownership or rights to a specific underlying asset, such as real estate, equity, or debt. Their significance lies in the potential to revolutionize traditional financial markets through asset tokenization. By converting physical assets into digital tokens, security tokens unlock liquidity, fractional ownership, and global accessibility. While the regulatory landscape for security tokens is still evolving, their potential to democratize investment and enhance market efficiency is compelling.

Central Bank Digital Currencies (CBDCs) represent the digital incarnation of a nation's fiat currency, issued and regulated by central banks. Their significance lies in the potential to modernize and innovate the financial system. CBDCs can streamline cross-border transactions, reduce costs, and provide greater financial inclusion. However, they also raise concerns about privacy, surveillance, and the impact on traditional banking systems.

In conclusion, the myriad types of cryptocurrencies underscore the remarkable diversity and innovation within the digital economy. From Bitcoin's foundational role to the specialized functionalities of privacy coins, utility tokens, and beyond, each type of cryptocurrency contributes to the evolving narrative of decentralized finance. As technology advances and the regulatory landscape matures, the significance of these digital assets is poised to shape the financial world, offering new possibilities for economic empowerment, technological progress, and financial inclusivity.

Introduction to cryptocurrency exchanges

In the digital age, the concept of value exchange has transcended physical boundaries, finding its manifestation in the realm of cryptocurrencies. Cryptocurrency exchanges are central to the vibrant ecosystem of digital assets, which facilitate the buying, selling, and trading of various cryptocurrencies. This section delves into the essential role of cryptocurrency exchanges, exploring their types, functionalities, significance, and the evolving landscape they navigate.

Exchanges for cryptocurrencies act as a bridge between established financial institutions and the emerging world of digital currencies. These platforms enable individuals and institutions to convert fiat currency, such as US dollars or euros, into cryptocurrencies like Bitcoin, Ethereum, etc. At its core, a cryptocurrency exchange provides a marketplace where buyers and sellers can interact, determining the price of various assets through supply and demand dynamics.

Cryptocurrency exchanges come in various forms, each catering to different user preferences and requirements. Centralized exchanges (CEXs) are the most common, characterized by a central governing entity that manages transactions, order matching, and custody of assets. While CEXs offer convenience and liquidity, they also come with centralized control, raising concerns about security breaches and the potential for manipulation.

On the other hand, decentralized exchanges (DEXs) operate without a central authority. They rely on smart contracts and blockchain technology to facilitate peer-to-peer trading directly between users. DEXs prioritize user control and security, as traders retain control of their private keys and assets. However, they often face challenges related to liquidity and user experience.

The functionality of cryptocurrency exchanges extends beyond the basic buying and selling of assets. These platforms offer various trading options, including limit orders, market orders, and stop orders, allowing users to execute trades at desired price levels. Additionally, advanced trading features like margin trading, futures contracts, and options enable traders to engage in more sophisticated strategies, amplifying potential gains while exposing them to increased risk.

Security is paramount in the cryptocurrency exchange landscape. Reputed exchanges implement robust security measures such as two-factor authentication (2FA), cold storage of funds, regular security audits, and multi-signature wallets to safeguard users' assets. Despite these measures, security breaches have occurred, emphasizing the necessity of exercising caution when choosing an exchange.

Cryptocurrency exchanges are pivotal in driving adoption and liquidity within the digital economy. They provide newcomers with a gateway to enter the world of cryptocurrencies by facilitating the purchase of digital assets using traditional fiat currencies. Moreover, exchanges contribute to price discovery, enabling users to gauge market sentiment and trends based on trading volumes and price movements.

Beyond individual traders, exchanges are essential for institutional participation in the cryptocurrency market. Exchanges are used by institutions, like hedge funds and asset managers, to carry out massive trades and manage portfolios. The emergence of regulated exchanges has further paved the way for institutional involvement, increasing the market's legitimacy and attracting more investors.

The landscape of cryptocurrency exchanges continues to evolve, driven by technological advancements, regulatory developments, and market trends. Regulatory compliance has become a focal point, with exchanges navigating a complex web of legal frameworks across different jurisdictions. Moreover, the emergence of decentralized finance (DeFi) has introduced the concept of decentralized exchanges (DEXs), which aim to address some of the shortcomings of traditional exchanges by prioritizing user control and privacy.

In conclusion, cryptocurrency exchanges serve as the bedrock of the digital asset ecosystem, offering users a means to participate in the transformative world of cryptocurrencies. Whether centralized or decentralized, these platforms facilitate the seamless exchange of value and information, shaping the future of finance and revolutionizing how individuals and institutions engage with digital assets. As the industry matures and technology advances, cryptocurrency exchanges remain pivotal in driving innovation, accessibility, and inclusivity in the global financial landscape.

CHAPTER II

Fundamentals of Trading

Basics of trading: buy, sell, and hold

In the intricate landscape of cryptocurrency trading, mastering the fundamentals is akin to equipping oneself with a compass for navigating the tumultuous waters of the digital asset market. At its core, crypto trading revolves around three fundamental actions: buying, selling, and holding. This section delves into the basics of these strategies, exploring their nuances, the factors that influence decision-making, and the significance of adopting a balanced approach to trading success.

Buying cryptocurrencies marks the initiation of a trading journey, and its timing is pivotal. Many traders aim to purchase assets at a relatively low price, anticipating future price appreciation. This practice aligns with the age-old adage "buy low, sell high." However, accurately timing the market is a challenge even for experienced traders, given the inherent volatility of the cryptocurrency market.

Various strategies are employed when buying cryptocurrencies. Swing traders seek short- to medium-term gains by capitalizing on price fluctuations. They analyze technical indicators, chart patterns, and market sentiment to identify optimal entry points. On the other hand, long-term investors, often referred to as "HODLers" (a term derived from a misspelling of "hold"), take a more patient approach. They believe in the long-term potential of a cryptocurrency, focusing on its underlying technology and fundamentals rather than short-term price movements.

Selling cryptocurrencies is driven by the pursuit of profits and the mitigation of risk. The primary goal is to sell assets higher than the purchase price, realizing a profit. This requires understanding market trends and analysis to determine optimal exit points. However, a common pitfall is succumbing to greed and holding onto assets for too long, missing out on potential gains as market sentiment changes.

Managing risk is a critical aspect of selling. Traders often set stop-loss orders, automatically selling a cryptocurrency if its price falls below a predetermined threshold. This practice aims to limit losses if the market turns unfavorable. Similarly, take-profit orders automatically sell assets once they reach a specific price target, ensuring that gains are captured even if the trader is not actively monitoring the market.

Holding refers to retaining cryptocurrencies for an extended period, often years, with the belief that their value will appreciate over time. This strategy is grounded in the assumption that the inherent value of a cryptocurrency will eventually be recognized, leading to significant returns. While holding can be financially rewarding, it requires a thorough understanding of the cryptocurrency's fundamentals and long-term potential.

The case of Bitcoin has exemplified the philosophy of holding. Early adopters who held onto their Bitcoin despite multiple price fluctuations have witnessed substantial gains over the years. This strategy demands a firm conviction in the underlying technology, the broader vision of the cryptocurrency, and the ability to weather market downturns without succumbing to panic selling.

In the pursuit of trading success, a balanced approach is essential. Relying solely on one strategy can expose traders to unnecessary risks. Diversification, the practice of spreading investments across different cryptocurrencies, trading strategies, and time horizons, is a cornerstone of risk management. It mitigates the impact of losses in one asset by leveraging gains in others, ensuring a more stable portfolio.

Furthermore, keeping emotions in check is crucial in executing effective trading strategies. Emotional decisions can lead to impulsive buying or selling, undermining the rationale behind trading actions. A disciplined mindset grounded in thorough analysis and a well-defined trading plan is paramount for sustained success in the volatile cryptocurrency market.

In conclusion, the basics of crypto trading revolve around buying, selling, and holding strategies. Each action requires a deep understanding of market dynamics, analysis techniques, and risk management principles. While buying marks the initiation of a trading journey, selling is driven by the pursuit of profits and risk mitigation. Holding, as a long-term investment philosophy, demands conviction and patience. A balanced approach, underpinned by diversification and disciplined decision-making, is the compass that guides traders through the unpredictable waters of the cryptocurrency market. As the industry continues to evolve, mastering these fundamentals remains an essential step in pursuing trading success.

Introduction to market orders, limit orders, and stop orders

In the dynamic landscape of cryptocurrency trading, success hinges upon mastering various order types that empower traders to execute transactions with precision and strategy. Market orders, limit orders, and stop orders represent cornerstones of this toolkit, offering distinct functionalities that cater to different trading objectives. This section explores these order types in-depth, elucidating their mechanics, applications, advantages, and potential pitfalls in pursuing profitable trading outcomes.

Market orders are the simplest and most direct way to execute a trade. A market order is a request made by a trader to buy or sell a certain amount of cryptocurrency at the current price. The allure of market orders lies in their swiftness and certainty of execution. These orders prioritize immediacy, making them suitable for situations where speed is crucial, such as taking advantage of short-lived price discrepancies or entering a trade without delay.

However, the flip side of market orders is that the exact execution price is not guaranteed. In highly volatile markets, the price at which a market order is executed can deviate from the displayed price due to rapid price fluctuations. This phenomenon, called slippage, can result in unintended costs or missed opportunities, especially during extreme volatility or low liquidity.

Limit orders offer traders greater control over the execution price, enabling them to set specific price thresholds at which they are willing to buy or sell a cryptocurrency. When placing a buy limit order, the trader specifies a price lower than the current market price. Conversely, a sell limit order is set above the current market price. The limit order is triggered and executed once the market reaches the specified price level.

The primary advantage of limit orders is the potential to obtain a more favorable execution price than what is currently available in the market. Traders can capitalize on price fluctuations to secure better deals. However, there is a trade-off between the price and the execution certainty. If the market fails to reach the specified price, the limit order may remain unexecuted, causing the trader to miss out on potential gains.

Stop orders are instrumental in managing risk and protecting profits in the cryptocurrency market. They serve as defensive tools by activating an order when the market price reaches a predetermined level, known as the stop price. Stop-limit orders and stop-loss orders are the two primary types of stop orders.

A stop-loss order limits potential losses by triggering a market order when the price falls to or below the stop price. This prevents further losses by ensuring a prompt exit from a losing trade. A stop-limit order, on the other hand, combines the characteristics of a stop order along with a limit order. It triggers a limit order when the market price reaches the stop price. While this adds a layer of control, it also carries the risk of the limit order not being executed if the market moves too rapidly.

Each order type has its unique applications and advantages, and traders often employ a combination of these orders to achieve specific trading objectives. For instance, a trader may use a limit order to buy at a lower price during a dip, while simultaneously setting a stop-loss order to minimize potential losses. Additionally, stop orders can be used to capitalize on market momentum, triggering buy orders when prices break through key resistance levels.

A successful trading strategy requires a nuanced understanding of these order types and their interplay. Traders must consider market conditions, volatility, trading volume, and risk tolerance when choosing which order type to employ. Moreover, continuously monitoring and adjusting orders in response to changing market dynamics is crucial to adapting and optimizing trading strategies over time.

In conclusion, market orders, limit orders, and stop orders are indispensable tools that empower traders to execute transactions with precision and strategy in the cryptocurrency market. Market orders prioritize speed of execution but come with the caveat of potential slippage. Limit orders offer control over execution prices, enabling traders to capitalize on price fluctuations, while stop orders provide risk management mechanisms to protect profits and minimize losses. A well-rounded trading strategy involves a thoughtful combination of these order types tailored to the trader's objectives and market analysis. As cryptocurrency markets evolve, mastering these order types remains a cornerstone of successful trading endeavors.

Risk management strategies for trading

In the exhilarating world of cryptocurrency trading, potential rewards often come hand in hand with inherent risks. As traders venture into this volatile landscape, implementing robust risk management strategies becomes paramount to safeguarding capital and achieving long-term success. This section delves into the intricacies of risk management, exploring key principles, methodologies, and practical techniques that traders can employ to navigate the cryptocurrency market safely and mitigate potential losses.

Risk, in the context of trading, refers to the possibility of experiencing financial losses due to adverse market movements. The volatile nature of the cryptocurrency market accentuates the importance of recognizing and quantifying risk. Traders must embrace the reality that even the most well-thought-out strategies can result in losses, and thus, managing risk is not only prudent but essential.

Position sizing is a fundamental risk management technique determining the amount of capital allocated to each trade. It involves calculating the ideal trade size based on account size, risk tolerance, and the distance between the entry and stop-loss points. By limiting the size of each trade relative to the overall trading capital, position sizing helps mitigate the impact of individual losses on the trader's portfolio.

The "2% rule" is a commonly cited guideline for position sizing, advocating for risking a maximum of 2% of the trading capital on any single trade. This approach prevents catastrophic losses that could cripple a trader's account and provides a buffer to recover from potential setbacks.

Stop-loss and take-profit levels are critical risk mitigation and profit protection tools. A stop-loss order is placed below the entry price at a predetermined price level, ensuring that losses are limited to a specific percentage of the trading capital. This prevents emotional decision-making in the heat of market fluctuations and curbs the potential for significant drawdowns.

Conversely, a take-profit order defines a price level at which a trade will be automatically exited to capture profits. This tool helps traders secure gains and avoid holding onto positions for too long, potentially giving back profits due to market reversals.

The risk-reward ratio is a critical metric that quantifies the potential reward against the possible loss in a trade. It helps traders assess whether a trade is worth pursuing based on its potential profit relative to the risk taken. As a general guideline, you should aim for a ratio of risk to reward of at least 1:2, which means that the possible return should be at least two times as great as the potential risk.

By consistently adhering to a favorable risk-reward ratio, traders can absorb losses from unsuccessful trades while still achieving profitability over the long term. This disciplined approach guards against the psychological pitfalls of overtrading or chasing unrealistic profits.

Diversification is a tried-and-true risk management strategy that spreads trading capital across different assets or markets. Trading professionals lessen the effect of poor performance in one asset on the entire portfolio by avoiding overconcentration in a single cryptocurrency. Diversification can also extend to trading strategies, ensuring that various approaches are employed to mitigate the effects of changing market conditions.

However, it's essential to strike a balance between diversification and over-diversification. Over-diversification can dilute potential gains and make tracking and managing many positions challenging.

While risk management techniques focus on quantitative aspects, emotional control is an often-underestimated component of risk management. Fear, greed, and impatience are a few examples of emotions that might cause impulsive decisions which deviate from a clearly laid out trading plan. Maintaining emotional discipline, sticking to pre-established risk parameters, and avoiding "revenge trading" after losses are essential aspects of risk management.

In conclusion, risk management strategies are the foundation for successful cryptocurrency trading. Position sizing, stop-loss and take-profit levels, risk-reward ratios, diversification, and emotional control collectively mitigate the inherent risks of trading and ensure long-term viability. Embracing risk management preserves capital and cultivates a disciplined and calculated approach to trading in the ever-fluctuating cryptocurrency market. As traders navigate the uncertainties of this dynamic landscape, applying these strategies can provide a solid foundation for profitable and sustainable trading endeavors.

Psychology of trading: managing emotions and mindset

In the fast-paced world of cryptocurrency trading, success is not solely determined by market analysis and technical skills. The psychology of trading plays a pivotal role in shaping outcomes, as emotions and mindset significantly impact decision-making and overall trading performance. This section delves into the intricate interplay between psychology and trading, exploring the emotions traders often grapple with, their psychological challenges, and strategies for cultivating a resilient mindset that fosters disciplined and effective trading.

Emotions are inherent to human nature and can either empower or undermine a trader's decision-making process. Greed, fear, overconfidence, and impatience are some of the emotions that traders frequently encounter. Greed may drive traders to chase high-risk opportunities for quick gains, while fear can lead to hesitancy or impulsive exits from trades. Overconfidence can result in excessive risk-taking, and impatience can lead traders to abandon well-thought-out strategies prematurely.

Acknowledging the presence of emotions is crucial, as ignoring or suppressing them can result in impulsive and irrational decision-making. The key is to recognize these emotions, understand their impact on decision-making, and develop strategies to manage them effectively.

Trading poses unique psychological challenges due to its uncertainty and the potential for financial gains and losses. One of the most significant challenges is dealing with losses. Loss aversion, the tendency to experience loss more painfully than gain, can cause emotional distress and impair logical decision-making. Traders often struggle to cut their losses, leading to "holding onto losers" and increasing the potential for more significant losses.

Another challenge is confirmation bias, where traders seek information confirming their beliefs and ignore contradictory evidence. This bias can lead to tunnel vision and prevent traders from objectively analyzing market data.

Developing a resilient trading mindset is essential for managing emotions and navigating the psychological challenges of trading. One fundamental principle is to separate self-worth from trading outcomes. Traders often tie their self-esteem to their performance in the market, which can lead to emotional volatility. Embracing a growth mindset, where learning from mistakes and continuous improvement are prioritized, can mitigate the impact of losses on self-esteem.

Additionally, traders should establish a well-defined trading plan that outlines entry and exit strategies, risk parameters, and overall goals. Following a plan reduces the influence of impulsive emotions during moments of uncertainty and market volatility.

The capacity to identify, comprehend, and control one's own emotions as well as those of others is known as emotional intelligence (EI). In trading, EI is crucial for making rational decisions and managing stress. EI empowers traders to remain calm in the face of market fluctuations and make decisions grounded in analysis rather than emotional impulses.

Traders can improve their emotional intelligence (EI) by engaging in mindfulness exercises like meditation and deep breathing. These techniques help regulate emotions, reduce stress, and improve focus, all essential for effective decision-making.

Cognitive biases are inherent mental shortcuts that can lead to distorted judgment and decision-making. Traders should be aware of biases such as hindsight bias, where they believe they "knew it all along" after the fact, and recency bias, where recent events outsize decision-making. Developing awareness of these biases and consistently challenging assumptions through objective analysis can help mitigate their impact.

In conclusion, the psychology of trading is an intricate interplay of emotions, mindset, and cognitive biases that significantly influence decision-making and overall trading performance. Managing emotions such as greed, fear, overconfidence, and impatience is essential for rational decisions. Psychological challenges, including loss aversion and confirmation bias, can impede effective trading. Cultivating a resilient trading mindset, focusing on emotional intelligence, and recognizing cognitive biases empower traders to make disciplined and rational choices in the face of market uncertainty. As traders continue to navigate the cryptocurrency landscape, honing their psychological skills is as essential as mastering technical analysis and market strategies.

CHAPTER III

Technical Analysis

Introduction to technical analysis

In cryptocurrency trading, understanding the ebb and flow of market trends is a pivotal skill. Technical analysis is a time-tested methodology that empowers traders to decipher market behavior by studying historical price and volume data. This section delves into the foundational principles of technical analysis, exploring its core concepts, tools, and significance in navigating the cryptocurrency market with insight and strategy.

At the heart of technical analysis lies the principle that price encompasses all available information. Unlike fundamental analysis, which delves into the intrinsic value of assets based on economic indicators and news events, technical analysis focuses solely on historical price and volume data. Traders believe past price movements reflect market sentiment and can offer valuable insights into potential future price movements.

Chart patterns are the visual representation of market psychology in action. These patterns emerge as traders' collective behavior drives price movements. Common chart patterns include trendlines, channels, triangles, and head and shoulders patterns. By identifying these patterns, traders can forecast probable price breakouts or reversals, creating opportunities for strategic entry and exit. Trendlines, for instance, are drawn by connecting consecutive lows in an uptrend or consecutive highs in a downtrend. These lines provide insights into the prevailing market direction and can serve as dynamic support or resistance levels.

Technical indicators are mathematical calculations that provide additional insights into market trends and potential reversals. These tools are superimposed onto price charts to help traders identify momentum, volatility, and other crucial metrics. Moving averages, RSI (Relative Strength Index), and MACD (Moving Average Convergence Divergence) are among the most widely used indicators. Moving averages, for instance, smooth out price fluctuations to reveal the underlying trend. The intersection of short-term and the long-term moving averages can signal potential trend changes.

Support and resistance levels are vital concepts in technical analysis. Support is a price level at which a cryptocurrency tends to stop falling and may even bounce back. Resistance, on the other hand, is a price level where a cryptocurrency tends to stop rising and may reverse its direction. These levels are identified based on historical price movements and can provide insights into potential entry and exit points. The breakout of a resistance level can signal a likely upward trend continuation, while a breakdown of a support level can indicate a possible downward trend continuation.

Candlestick patterns visually represent price movements within a specified time frame. Each candlestick provides information about an asset's opening, closing, high, and low prices. By analyzing candlestick patterns, traders can gain insights into market sentiment and potential trend reversals. Patterns such as doji, engulfing, and hammer can provide valuable clues about shifts in market dynamics. For instance, a doji, which appears after a significant price movement, denotes uncertainty and a probable trend reversal.

Successful application of technical analysis requires a holistic approach that integrates multiple tools and concepts. Traders often begin by identifying the prevailing trend using moving averages or trendlines. They then analyze chart patterns and indicators to confirm their analysis and identify potential entry or exit points. Additionally, timeframes play a crucial role in technical analysis. Different timeframes, such as daily, hourly, or even minute-based charts, provide different insights into market trends. Short-term traders may focus on lower timeframes for quick entries and exits, while long-term investors may rely on higher timeframes for trend identification.

In conclusion, technical analysis is both an art and a science that empowers traders to decode market trends, patterns, and sentiments. By studying historical price and volume data, traders gain insights into potential future price movements, enabling them to make informed decisions about entries, exits, and risk management. Chart patterns, indicators, support and resistance levels, candlestick patterns, and trendlines collectively form the technical analysis toolkit. As traders continue to navigate the ever-evolving landscape of cryptocurrency trading, a well-rounded understanding of technical analysis can serve as a compass, guiding them through the complexities of the market with enhanced insight and strategy.

Key technical indicators (moving averages, RSI, MACD, etc.)

In cryptocurrency trading, understanding market dynamics goes beyond surface-level observation. Key technical indicators are essential tools that empower traders to delve deeper into price movements, trends, and momentum. Moving averages, Relative Strength Index (RSI), Moving Average Convergence Divergence (MACD), and other such indicators serve as analytical instruments that offer valuable insights into the ever-evolving cryptocurrency market landscape. This section comprehensively explores these key technical indicators, elucidating their mechanics, interpretation, and significance in shaping trading strategies and decision-making.

Moving averages are foundational indicators that provide a smoothed representation of price data over a specific period. These indicators help traders identify trends by eliminating short-term fluctuations and highlighting the underlying direction of the market. Two common types of moving averages are the SMA (Simple Moving Average) and EMA (Exponential Moving Average). SMA generates a consistent perspective of price trends by calculating the average price over a predetermined number of periods. However, the EMA is more responsive to short-term price changes since it gives current prices greater weight. Moving averages are frequently used by traders to spot trend changes, crossovers between short- and long-term averages, and possible support and resistance levels.

A momentum oscillator called Relative Strength Index (RSI) measures how quickly and dramatically price movements change. It is utilized to determine whether the market is overbought or oversold and has a scale from 0 to 100. RSI allows traders to assess the strength of a trend and probable reversal points by comparing the size of current gains to current losses. An RSI value above 70 suggests overbought conditions, indicating a potential reversal or price correction. Conversely, an RSI value below 30 means oversold conditions, indicating a possible upward bounce. Traders often look for divergence between price and RSI, as divergences can signal momentum shifts.

Moving Average Convergence Divergence, also known as MACD is a versatile indicator combining moving averages and momentum concepts. It consists of two components: the MACD line and the signal line. The difference between two moving averages—typically the 12-period EMA and the 26-period EMA—is what makes up the MACD line. The MACD line's 9-period EMA serves as the signal line. The MACD offers information on trend momentum and possible crossovers. A bullish signal, which denotes possible upward momentum, is generated when the MACD line passes above the signal line. In contrast, a bearish signal is produced when the MACD line passes below the signal line, indicating probable downward momentum. The MACD histogram, which depicts the variation between the MACD line and the signal line, offers graphical indicators of the momentum's strength.

Bollinger Bands are made up of three lines: an upper and a lower band that are normally two standard deviations distant from the middle band, and the middle band (often a 20-period SMA). Bollinger Bands serve as a tool to measure volatility and price range. When the price goes toward the upper band, it suggests that the market is overbought, potentially signaling a reversal or price correction. Conversely, when the price moves toward the lower band, it means that the market is oversold, indicating a potential upward bounce. Traders often look for price breakouts beyond the bands, as these breakouts can signal strong trends or momentum shifts.

Effective utilization of these key technical indicators involves harmonizing insights from multiple tools. For instance, traders may use moving averages to identify trends, RSI to assess momentum, and MACD to confirm crossovers and potential trend changes. Combining these indicators enhances the reliability of trading signals and decision-making. It's important to note that no single indicator is infallible, and traders should avoid relying solely on one indicator. Market conditions can change rapidly, and the interplay of various indicators provides a more comprehensive view of the evolving landscape.

In conclusion, key technical indicators are the compasses that guide traders through the intricate landscape of cryptocurrency trading. Moving averages illuminate trends, RSI quantifies momentum, MACD unifies momentum and trend, and Bollinger Bands measure volatility and price range. By skillfully integrating insights from these indicators, traders can make informed decisions about entries, exits, and risk management, ultimately enhancing their precision and effectiveness in the market. As the cryptocurrency market evolves, these technical indicators remain essential tools that empower traders to navigate with insight and strategy to pursue trading success.

Chart patterns and their interpretations

In cryptocurrency trading, where volatility and rapid price fluctuations are the norm, traders often rely on technical analysis to gain insights into potential price movements. Chart patterns stand out as visual representations of market psychology and trends among the diverse tools and techniques within technical analysis.

Chart patterns are visual formations that emerge on price charts over time, reflecting the collective behavior of market participants. They provide insights into the balance between supply and demand, offering traders a glimpse into potential future price movements. By recognizing these patterns, traders can anticipate shifts in market sentiment and position themselves to capitalize on emerging opportunities.

Two primary categories of chart patterns exist: continuation patterns and reversal patterns. Continuation patterns, including flags, pennants, and triangles, suggest a temporary pause in the ongoing trend before it resumes. These formations often signify a consolidation phase within a prevailing trend, highlighting potential areas of price stability before further movement.

On the other hand, reversal patterns hint at a potential change in the existing trend. Examples of reversal patterns include the head and shoulders pattern, double top and double bottom patterns, and triple top and triple bottom patterns. For instance, the head and shoulders pattern consists of three distinct peaks, with the central peak being the highest. This pattern is widely regarded as a signal of a trend reversal—a shift from an uptrend to a downtrend, or vice versa for the inverse head and shoulders.

Interpreting chart patterns involves deciphering the underlying psychology of market participants. A symmetrical triangle pattern, characterized by converging trendlines, suggests indecision and the potential for a breakout in either direction. Conversely, a descending triangle pattern, formed by a horizontal support level and a declining trendline, hints at increased selling pressure.

Traders must consider the pattern's context, timeframe, and volume alongside other technical indicators to arrive at a comprehensive interpretation. The efficacy of chart patterns lies in their ability to visually represent complex market dynamics, aiding traders in making informed decisions.

Leveraging chart patterns in cryptocurrency trading involves several strategic considerations. Firstly, these patterns can confirm existing trends, helping traders determine whether a trend is likely to continue or if a reversal might occur. Secondly, chart patterns offer entry and exit points. Breakouts from consolidation patterns provide favorable entry opportunities, while recognizing reversal patterns early can help traders exit positions before a trend reversal becomes evident.

Additionally, chart patterns aid in risk management. Traders can strategically place stop-loss levels based on pattern breakouts, minimizing potential losses in the event of adverse price movements. Combining multiple chart patterns and technical indicators provides a comprehensive market view, increasing confidence in trading decisions.

It's important to note that the timeframe of a chart pattern matters. Patterns observed on shorter timeframes may have different implications than those on longer ones. Traders must adapt their interpretations accordingly, considering the context in which a pattern emerges.

In conclusion, chart patterns serve as a visual language in cryptocurrency trading, offering insights into market sentiment, trends, and potential turning points. While not foolproof predictors of future price movements, these patterns provide a structured framework for analysis. Successful interpretation requires combining technical expertise, risk management, and a deep understanding of market dynamics. By incorporating chart patterns into their trading arsenal, cryptocurrency traders can navigate the complex landscape with greater precision, improving their ability to identify opportunities and manage risks effectively.

Applying technical analysis to cryptocurrency markets

The cryptocurrency market, marked by its volatility and rapid price fluctuations, presents a unique canvas for traders to apply technical analysis. The principles and tools of technical analysis, honed through decades of traditional market analysis, find new relevance in this digital realm. This section delves into the art and science of applying technical analysis to cryptocurrency markets, exploring the nuances, challenges, and strategies traders employ to navigate this dynamic landscape with insight and precision.

While cryptocurrencies represent a novel asset class, the underlying principles of technical analysis remain unchanged. The essence lies in interpreting historical price and volume data to identify patterns, trends, and potential future price movements. Market sentiment, shaped by the collective emotions of traders, is reflected in these price movements, making technical analysis a tool to decipher the digital pulse of the cryptocurrency market.

Volatility is both a hallmark and a challenge in cryptocurrency markets. While it presents opportunities for rapid profit generation, it also amplifies the risks of unexpected reversals. The technical analysis becomes a formidable ally in understanding and capitalizing on this volatility. Moving averages, for instance, smooth out price fluctuations, helping traders identify the underlying trend amidst the chaos. Cryptocurrencies are known for their ability to trend strongly, and trend-following strategies are particularly relevant in such markets. Applying moving averages, trendlines, and other indicators aids in identifying and riding these trends, whether they are short-term swings or more extended bull or bear markets.

Like traditional markets, cryptocurrency markets benefit from the interplay of multiple indicators. For instance, a trader may use the RSI which is also known as Relative Strength Index to determine overbought or oversold conditions, providing insights into potential reversals. Simultaneously, they could analyze chart patterns to corroborate the RSI's signals and provide additional context to the analysis. The Moving Average Convergence Divergence (MACD), a versatile tool, can help confirm trend reversals, identify momentum shifts, and highlight potential entry and exit points. Combining the insights from RSI and MACD enhances the trader's understanding of the market dynamics.

Cryptocurrency markets operate 24/7, unlike traditional markets that have defined trading hours. This constant activity requires traders to adapt their technical analysis strategies for round-the-clock price movements. Continuation patterns like flags and pennants can provide valuable insights into potential price movements even when the sun never sets on the cryptocurrency market. Moreover, sentiment plays a profound role in cryptocurrency markets. News, social media chatter, and regulatory developments can lead to rapid shifts in sentiment and price. Traders must incorporate sentiment and technical analyses to gain a holistic view of market dynamics.

Cryptocurrency markets are not immune to false signals generated by technical indicators. These false signals can result from sudden price spikes, low liquidity, or market manipulation. Traders must exercise caution and avoid making impulsive decisions based solely on one indicator. Confirmation becomes a key strategy for managing false signals. Multiple indicators pointing in the same direction, alongside a supportive market context and volume trends, can validate the signals generated by a single indicator. Waiting for confirmation reduces the risk of acting on misleading signals.

Applying technical analysis goes beyond the tools, including meticulous risk management and position sizing. Cryptocurrency markets' volatility can lead to unexpected outcomes, underscoring the importance of setting stop-loss and take-profit levels. Position sizing ensures that losses from unsuccessful trades do not disproportionately impact the trader's capital. Due to the potential for rapid price swings, traders must balance capital preservation and risk-taking.

In conclusion, applying technical analysis to cryptocurrency markets combines art, science, tradition, and innovation. As traders navigate cryptocurrencies' volatile and ever-changing landscape, technical analysis becomes a guiding light that illuminates the terrain and offers insights into market trends, sentiment, and potential price movements. The principles of interpreting historical price and volume data, recognizing chart patterns, and using indicators hold true in this digital realm, albeit with considerations specific to cryptocurrencies. Through a multidimensional approach, confirmation strategies, and sound risk management, traders can harness the power of technical analysis to navigate the complexities of cryptocurrency markets and make informed decisions that align with their trading objectives.

CHAPTER IV

Fundamental Analysis

Introduction to fundamental analysis

Cryptocurrency trading is a dynamic landscape characterized by rapid price fluctuations, emerging trends, and an intricate interplay of factors that influence market sentiment. While technical analysis is a well- known approach to deciphering price movements, fundamental analysis offers a deeper understanding of the underlying factors that drive cryptocurrency values.

Fundamental analysis is an approach employed to evaluate the intrinsic value of an asset by scrutinizing the underlying factors that influence its price. In the context of cryptocurrencies, this approach aims to uncover the key drivers that impact the value of digital assets, going beyond price charts and technical indicators.

Cryptocurrency markets are unique in their susceptibility to external factors influencing price movements. While sentiment, speculation, and market psychology play pivotal roles, fundamental analysis offers a grounding force by examining the fundamental attributes of a cryptocurrency. Traders relying solely on technical analysis may be unprepared for market shocks caused by regulatory developments, technological advancements, partnerships, and macroeconomic trends.

The fundamental analysis comprises various components that collectively provide a holistic view of a cryptocurrency's value. These components include technology and innovation, market adoption, regulatory landscape, market sentiment, economic factors, and the team and leadership behind a project. Evaluating these factors equips traders with a comprehensive understanding of the cryptocurrency's potential for growth and sustainability.

To effectively apply fundamental analysis, traders must develop a multifaceted skill set. Thorough research, staying updated on news and events, and understanding the broader economic landscape are foundational. Analyzing whitepapers, scrutinizing project roadmaps, and participating in relevant online communities contribute to a well-rounded perspective. Traders must also be prepared to synthesize information from various sources, as the interplay of fundamental factors is often intricate and nuanced.

Fundamental analysis serves as a compass for cryptocurrency traders navigating an ever-changing landscape. Traders can make informed decisions beyond short-term price movements by understanding the technological, economic, and social factors that shape cryptocurrency values. While fundamental analysis may not provide pinpoint accuracy in predicting price fluctuations, it empowers traders with the insights needed to identify potential opportunities, manage risk, and cultivate a long-term perspective.

In conclusion, fundamental analysis serves as a crucial tool for cryptocurrency traders seeking to navigate the complexities of the market. By diving deep into the intrinsic factors that drive cryptocurrency values, traders can enhance their decision-making processes and position themselves for success in a dynamic and evolving landscape.

Factors affecting cryptocurrency prices (regulation, adoption, partnerships, etc.)

The cryptocurrency market, characterized by its volatility and rapid price movements, operates within a dynamic ecosystem influenced by an intricate interplay of factors. Beyond the traditional forces that shape financial markets, cryptocurrencies are subject to a unique set of variables that drive price fluctuations. This section delves into the multifaceted tapestry of factors affecting cryptocurrency prices, ranging from regulatory developments and adoption trends to technological innovations and market sentiment. By understanding these dynamics, traders and investors can navigate the complexities of the cryptocurrency landscape with insight and strategy.

Regulation is a dominant force in the cryptocurrency market, profoundly impacting prices and market sentiment. The evolving regulatory landscape varies across jurisdictions, ranging from welcoming environments that foster innovation to stringent frameworks that curtail cryptocurrency activities. The announcement of regulatory measures can lead to price swings, as investors react to changes in the legality, taxation, and trading of cryptocurrencies.

Positive regulatory developments, such as recognizing cryptocurrencies as legitimate assets, can bolster investor confidence and drive prices upward. Conversely, restrictive measures, like bans or strict Know Your Customer (KYC) regulations, can trigger sell-offs and market uncertainty. As global regulators seek to balance innovation and consumer protection, their decisions will continue to shape the cryptocurrency market's trajectory.

The adoption of cryptocurrencies for real-world applications is a pivotal factor that influences their value. Cryptocurrencies gain value when they demonstrate utility beyond speculative trading. Use cases such as decentralized finance (DeFi), non-fungible tokens (NFTs), and cross-border remittances showcase the potential for cryptocurrencies to revolutionize industries and provide tangible benefits.

Increased adoption by businesses, merchants, and consumers fuels demand, driving up prices. For instance, partnerships between cryptocurrencies and established companies can boost confidence and encourage adoption. Conversely, a lack of real-world use cases and adoption challenges can hinder price growth. As the ecosystem expands and cryptocurrencies find more practical applications, adoption will remain a focal point for price dynamics.

Partnerships and collaborations are crucial in cryptocurrency, impacting technological advancements and price movements. Collaborations between blockchain projects, corporations, and institutions can lead to innovative solutions and increased credibility. When established players in traditional industries forge alliances with cryptocurrency projects, it signals mainstream acceptance and can drive significant price appreciation.

Partnerships also facilitate interoperability between different blockchain networks, enhancing cryptocurrencies' overall utility and value proposition. For example, interoperability between different blockchains can enable seamless asset transfers and access to decentralized applications (dApps), fostering a vibrant ecosystem and driving demand for associated tokens.

Market sentiment and speculation are inherent characteristics of the cryptocurrency market, driving rapid price fluctuations. Positive news, optimistic sentiment on social media, and mass media coverage can trigger buying frenzies, leading to rapid price increases. Conversely, negative news, security breaches, or regulatory uncertainties can lead to panic selling, resulting in price crashes.

The speculative nature of the market, where prices can be driven by herd behavior and fear of missing out (FOMO), underscores the importance of emotional resilience and risk management for traders and investors. While sentiment-driven price movements can offer lucrative opportunities, they also have inherent risks.

Innovation and advancements in technology are at the core of the cryptocurrency space. Updates, upgrades, and new protocols can significantly impact cryptocurrency prices. For instance, implementing scaling solutions, consensus algorithms, and privacy features can enhance the functionality and adoption of specific cryptocurrencies.

Forks, where a blockchain splits into two separate chains, can create new cryptocurrencies and alter market dynamics. A successful fork that addresses scalability or security concerns can attract attention and investment, potentially impacting the value of both the original and new cryptocurrencies.

Global economic trends, such as inflation, monetary policy shifts, and geopolitical events, have ripple effects that extend to the cryptocurrency market. Cryptocurrencies are increasingly viewed as alternative assets that can serve as a hedge against traditional market risks. In times of economic uncertainty, investors may flock to cryptocurrencies as a store of value, driving up prices.

Additionally, macro-economic factors influence market liquidity and capital flows. For instance, quantitative easing measures adopted by central banks can lead to increased liquidity in the markets, potentially finding their way into cryptocurrencies and driving price appreciation.

In conclusion, a complex network of factors that go beyond traditional financial markets affect the price dynamics of cryptocurrencies. Regulatory developments, adoption trends, partnerships, market sentiment, technological advancements, and macro-economic factors collectively contribute to the valuation of cryptocurrencies. Understanding these multifaceted dynamics becomes paramount for traders and investors seeking to navigate the market with insight and strategy as the cryptocurrency landscape continues to evolve. By analyzing these factors' interplay, cryptocurrency ecosystem participants can make educated decisions that align with their risk tolerance, investment goals, and time horizons.

Evaluating the whitepaper and project team

In the dynamic world of cryptocurrencies, where innovation and disruption intersect, the significance of evaluating investment opportunities cannot be overstated. Two fundamental pillars that underpin the decision-making process for investors are the project's whitepaper and the competency of its team. These elements serve as guideposts for assessing a cryptocurrency project's feasibility, potential, and credibility. This section delves into the art and science of evaluating the whitepaper and project team, exploring the nuances, methodologies, and considerations that empower investors to make knowledgeable decisions in the fast-paced and ever-evolving cryptocurrency landscape.

The whitepaper is the foundational document that outlines a cryptocurrency project's vision, purpose, mechanics, and technical details. Often authored by the project's creators, the whitepaper is akin to a blueprint that elucidates the problem the project aims to solve, its technological architecture, use cases, and potential impact on various industries. Investors turn to the whitepaper to understand the project's value proposition, innovation quotient, and potential to disrupt traditional sectors.

When evaluating a whitepaper, several key aspects come into play. Firstly, clarity and comprehensiveness are paramount. A well-structured whitepaper should clearly articulate the project's objectives, explain the technology underlying the cryptocurrency, and address potential challenges and solutions. A robust whitepaper also includes a detailed roadmap outlining the project's milestones, timelines, and deliverables. A solid roadmap demonstrates the project's commitment to development and its capacity to execute on its goals.

Furthermore, the technical aspects of the project outlined in the whitepaper should be coherent and feasible. Investors seek technical rigor, innovative solutions, and a deep understanding of the problem. A whitepaper that showcases technical prowess and originality garners confidence, as it suggests that the creators possess the expertise to implement their vision.

Beyond the whitepaper, the project team is a pivotal factor that shapes investors' perceptions of a cryptocurrency project's potential success. The team's competence, credibility, and experience collectively contribute to investors' confidence in the project's execution and ability to overcome challenges.

A well-rounded team comprises individuals with diverse skills that span technology, finance, marketing, and legal domains. For instance, a blockchain project necessitates a deep understanding of cryptography and distributed ledger technology. Meanwhile, a solid grasp of financial markets, regulations, and compliance ensures the project's alignment with legal frameworks and industry standards.

Team credibility and experience are also crucial. A team with a history of accomplished projects, industry acclaim, and subject-matter knowledge communicates competence and inspires trust in investors. Moreover, transparent communication and active engagement with the community underscore the team's commitment and accountability.

Transparency is a bedrock principle that fuels trust in the cryptocurrency space. Investors seek projects that embrace openness and provide timely updates on their progress. Communication channels such as official websites, social media platforms, and community forums enable investors to gauge the project's engagement, responsiveness, and commitment to sharing information.

A transparent project about its challenges, setbacks, and potential risks is forthcoming. Acknowledging vulnerabilities and addressing them head-on demonstrates integrity and helps manage expectations. Additionally, projects involving the community in decision-making foster a sense of ownership and collaboration, further enhancing trust.

Evaluating the whitepaper and project team requires a holistic approach beyond individual components. Investors must undertake due diligence that involves scrutinizing the alignment of the team's experience with the project's goals, cross-referencing claims in the whitepaper with technical feasibility, and assessing the project's positioning within the broader cryptocurrency landscape.

Moreover, risk assessment is a critical facet of the evaluation process. Investors must acknowledge that even the most promising projects carry inherent risks, such as regulatory uncertainties, technological vulnerabilities, or competitive challenges. By conducting a thorough risk analysis, investors can make educated decisions that align with their risk tolerance and investment objectives.

In conclusion, evaluating the whitepaper and project team represents a cornerstone of prudent cryptocurrency investment. The whitepaper serves as a roadmap for innovation, outlining the project's vision, technological architecture, and execution strategy. When assessing whitepapers, investors look for clarity, technical rigor, and a feasible roadmap. The project team, on the other hand, embodies the project's competence, credibility, and experience. A well-rounded team with diverse skills and a history of successful projects inspires confidence and trust.

Transparency, effective communication, due diligence, and risk assessment collectively form the toolkit that empowers investors to navigate the cryptocurrency landscape with insight and strategy. As the cryptocurrency ecosystem evolves, rigorous evaluation of projects becomes paramount for making informed investment decisions that align with risk tolerance, financial goals, and long-term aspirations. By mastering the art of assessing whitepapers and project teams, investors can venture into cryptocurrencies with confidence, empowerment, and preparedness.

Case studies of fundamental analysis in action

Fundamental analysis, the cornerstone methodology of evaluating investments based on underlying value, finds its application in cryptocurrencies as a guiding light for traders and investors. By delving into economic indicators, financial statements, adoption trends, and technological innovations, fundamental analysis uncovers the intrinsic worth of assets in a dynamic and ever- evolving landscape. This section explores real-world case studies that exemplify the power of fundamental analysis, showcasing its ability to unearth opportunities, predict trends, and inform strategic decisions in the intricate world of cryptocurrencies.

Case Study 1: Bitcoin's Meteoric Rise and Institutional Adoption

Bitcoin, the pioneering cryptocurrency, serves as a prime example of fundamental analysis in action. Its decentralized nature and limited supply underpin its value proposition. However, fundamental factors beyond the technology led to its meteoric rise.

In recent years, Bitcoin experienced growing institutional adoption. Corporations like MicroStrategy and Tesla allocated portions of their balance sheets to Bitcoin, signaling mainstream recognition and the adoption of cryptocurrencies as a store of value. Fundamental analysis was pivotal in assessing this adoption trend, considering factors such as regulatory environment, macroeconomic conditions, and the broader institutional landscape.

Additionally, the scarcity of Bitcoin, capped at 21 million coins, drove investor interest. Fundamental analysts scrutinized Bitcoin's monetary policy, comparing it to traditional fiat currencies subject to inflationary pressures. This evaluation of supply dynamics contributed to the narrative of Bitcoin as digital gold and influenced investor sentiment.

Case Study 2: DeFi's Disruption and Yield Farming Frenzy

Decentralized Finance (DeFi) represents another arena where fundamental analysis provides insights into the potential of new paradigms. DeFi projects offer financial services without intermediaries, revolutionizing traditional finance. One notable case study is the yield farming frenzy.

Yield farming involves liquidity provision to decentralized protocols in exchange for rewards. Fundamental analysis guided investors in evaluating the underlying mechanisms of DeFi protocols, understanding smart contract security, governance mechanisms, and the sustainability of reward distribution. By analyzing token economics and understanding the project's long-term vision, investors identified protocols with strong fundamentals that could weather market volatility.

Fundamental analysis also informed investors about the risks of impermanent loss, smart contract vulnerabilities, and the potential for unsustainable reward structures. Yield farming participants armed with fundamental insights made calculated decisions, choosing protocols that aligned with their risk tolerance and investment objectives.

Case Study 3: Ethereum's Technological Upgrades and EIP-1559

Ethereum, often called the "world computer," exemplifies how fundamental analysis encompasses technical and economic considerations. This fusion is made possible by Ethereum's switch from a PoW (Proof-of-Work) to a PoS (Proof-of-Stake) consensus mechanism, or Ethereum 2.0.

Fundamental analysts evaluated the technical feasibility of Ethereum 2.0, considering the benefits of scalability, security, and energy efficiency. However, the economic aspect also played a crucial role. Ethereum's shift to a Proof-of-Stake mechanism meant that Ether (ETH) holders could participate in staking and earn rewards. Fundamental analysis assessed the potential yield from staking, factoring in variables such as staking rewards, network congestion, and the demand for staked Ether.

Another notable development is Ethereum's EIP-1559 upgrade, which introduced a deflationary mechanism by burning transaction fees. Fundamental analysis delved into the implications of this upgrade on Ether's supply dynamics and its potential impact on price. Analysts weighed the supply reduction against the possible increase in demand due to improved transaction efficiency.

Case Study 4: NFTs and Cultural Significance Non-

Fungible Tokens (NFTs) emerged as a novel application of blockchain technology, underlining the role of fundamental analysis in assessing cultural and societal trends. NFTs represent ownership of unique digital assets like art, music, and collectibles. Fundamental analysis extends beyond financial considerations to evaluate the cultural significance of NFTs.

The Beeple case exemplifies this fusion of culture and finance. The price and cultural significance of Beeple's record-breaking selling of a digital collage for $69 million attracted media attention. Fundamental analysis encompassed factors such as the artist's reputation, the growth of digital art appreciation, and the broader adoption of NFTs in industries like gaming and music.

Investors who conducted thorough fundamental analysis recognized that the value of NFTs extended beyond financial returns. The potential for these tokens to reshape artistic expression and intellectual property ownership influenced investment decisions.

In conclusion, the case studies presented exemplify the art and science of fundamental analysis in the cryptocurrency ecosystem. From Bitcoin's institutional adoption to DeFi's yield farming frenzy, from Ethereum's technological upgrades to the cultural significance of NFTs, fundamental analysis unveils opportunities and mitigates risks. It involves evaluating technological and economic factors, societal trends, adoption dynamics, and regulatory shifts.

As cryptocurrency evolves, fundamental analysis remains a powerful tool for informed decision-making. By delving into the intrinsic value of assets, understanding the broader context, and navigating the complexities of the market with insight and strategy, traders and investors can make prudent choices that align with their risk tolerance and long-term objectives. The fusion of analysis, intuition, and a deep understanding of the fundamental landscape forms the backbone of successful cryptocurrency investment endeavors.

CHAPTER V

Sentiment Analysis

Understanding market sentiment

Cryptocurrency trading, a realm characterized by its volatility and rapid price movements, is often influenced by a powerful force that transcends traditional financial metrics—market sentiment. The emotional currents that shape price fluctuations in the cryptocurrency market can be challenging to decipher, yet understanding market sentiment is a crucial skill for traders seeking to navigate this dynamic landscape. This section delves into the intricate world of understanding market sentiment in cryptocurrency trading, exploring its nuances, methodologies, and significance in deciphering the emotional waves that drive price trends and inform trading decisions.

The cryptocurrency market stands apart from traditional financial markets due to its unique characteristics and market participants. Unlike conventional stocks or commodities, cryptocurrencies are relatively nascent assets influenced by many factors, including technological advancements, regulatory developments, adoption trends, and even social media discussions. As a result, market sentiment in the cryptocurrency space is subject to a high degree of volatility and can experience rapid shifts based on news and events.

Understanding market sentiment in cryptocurrency trading involves deciphering the emotional reactions of various participants, from retail investors to institutional traders, speculators to long-term holders. These participants bring their perceptions, biases, and emotions into the market, collectively shaping price movements.

Cryptocurrency market sentiment encompasses a range of emotions and attitudes that influence trading decisions. Fear and greed, two fundamental components of investor psychology, play a pivotal role. Fear can trigger panic selling during times of uncertainty or negative news, leading to price drops. Conversely, greed can drive FOMO (fear of missing out), causing traders to rush into buying assets during periods of rapid price appreciation.

News and social media discussions are potent contributors to sentiment. Positive news, technological upgrades, or partnership announcements can fuel optimism and drive bullish sentiment. On the other hand, negative news, regulatory crackdowns, or security breaches can breed pessimism and lead to bearish sentiment.

Moreover, sentiment indicators such as the Crypto Fear & Greed Index attempt to quantify market sentiment using various metrics, including price volatility, trading volume, social media discussions, and more. These indicators offer traders a glimpse into the collective emotional state of the market.

Market sentiment often gives rise to herding behavior, where traders follow the actions of the crowd rather than conducting independent analysis. This phenomenon can lead to exaggerated price movements driven by emotions rather than rational decision-making. For instance, during periods of FOMO, traders might jump into buying an asset solely based on its rapid price increase, without considering its fundamentals.

The cryptocurrency market exhibits particularly strong herding behavior because of its scale and the prominence of retail investors. This behavior can create feedback loops, where price movements trigger more traders to join the trend, intensifying the emotional-driven rally or sell-off.

Understanding market sentiment in cryptocurrency trading comes with challenges. The intangible nature of emotions makes quantifying sentiment a complex task. Sentiment indicators can provide insights but may not capture the full range of emotional currents. Moreover, sentiment can shift rapidly based on news or events, making real-time analysis a necessity.

Furthermore, market participants with vested interests can manipulate or distort sentiment. Pump-and-dump schemes take advantage of sentiment to increase profits by inflating asset prices artificially before selling them. False information or rumors spread through social media can distort sentiment and trigger unwarranted price movements.

Cryptocurrency trading strategies often involve a combination of technical and fundamental analysis. While technical analysis relies on price charts, patterns, and historical data, and fundamental analysis assesses the intrinsic value of an asset, sentiment analysis complements these methodologies by providing insights into the emotional drivers behind price movements.

However, sentiment analysis must be used cautiously. While sentiment-driven price movements can offer trading opportunities, they can also lead to losses if not combined with a strong understanding of technical and fundamental factors. Considering all three aspects, a balanced approach can lead to more informed and prudent trading decisions.

Traders can access various tools and strategies for understanding market sentiment in cryptocurrency trading. Social media platforms, online forums, and cryptocurrency news outlets can offer insights into ongoing discussions, opinions, and news events. Monitoring sentiment indicators like the Crypto Fear & Greed Index can provide a snapshot of the market's emotional state.

Additionally, sentiment analysis platforms use natural language processing algorithms to analyze news articles, social media posts, and other textual data to gauge sentiment. These platforms assign sentiment scores to different assets, indicating whether discussions are predominantly positive, negative, or neutral.

Understanding market sentiment also requires managing one's own emotions. Cryptocurrency trading can be emotionally taxing, as the market's rapid price fluctuations can trigger stress, anxiety, and impulsivity. Emotional discipline and psychological resilience are essential for traders to avoid rash decisions driven by fear or greed.

In conclusion, understanding market sentiment in cryptocurrency trading is a multifaceted endeavor that requires deciphering the emotional currents that drive price movements. The unique characteristics of the cryptocurrency market, coupled with the influence of news, social media, and herding behavior, create a dynamic landscape where sentiment plays a pivotal role.

Tools and methods for sentiment analysis

In the fast-paced and ever-evolving landscape of cryptocurrency trading, understanding market sentiment has emerged as a pivotal factor in making informed investment decisions. The rise of digital communication platforms, social media, and online forums has given birth to a digital echo chamber where traders, investors, and enthusiasts exchange opinions, news, and emotions that collectively shape the price movements of digital assets. This section delves into the array of tools and methods employed for sentiment analysis in crypto trading, shedding light on the technologies, strategies, and insights that empower traders to navigate market sentiment's complex and often unpredictable terrain.

The digital echo chamber serves as an arena where participants express their thoughts, share news, and engage in discussions that reverberate across the cryptocurrency community. This digital landscape encompasses social media platforms like Twitter, Reddit, Telegram, and online cryptocurrency forums. As traders and enthusiasts voice their opinions, fears, hopes, and predictions, they create a dynamic environment rich with emotional currents that can sway market sentiment.

Natural Language Processing (NLP) emerges as a potent tool for sentiment analysis in crypto trading. NLP leverages machine learning algorithms to analyze and understand human language. In sentiment analysis, NLP algorithms scrutinize social media posts, news articles, forum discussions, and comments to gauge the emotional tone behind the text.

Sentiment analysis using NLP involves classifying text into positive, negative, or neutral categories. NLP algorithms parse the content, identify keywords, phrases, and linguistic patterns indicative of sentiment, and assign a sentiment score to the text. These scores offer traders insights into the prevailing sentiment surrounding specific assets or the broader market.

Sentiment analysis platforms, powered by machine learning and NLP, provide traders with a systematic and automated approach to deciphering market sentiment. These platforms aggregate data from various sources, including social media, news articles, and forums, and analyze the text to assign sentiment scores to different assets.

Furthermore, sentiment analysis platforms provide nuanced insights beyond binary sentiment classifications. They may categorize sentiment as bullish, bearish, neutral, or even quantify the sentiment intensity on a scale. These platforms also allow traders to track sentiment trends over time, identifying shifts in market sentiment that could impact price movements.

Social media tracking tools enable traders to monitor real-time sentiment expressed on social media platforms. These tools scan platforms like Twitter for keywords, hashtags, and discussions related to specific cryptocurrencies. Social media tracking tools provide a snapshot of the prevailing sentiment by analyzing the frequency and context of these mentions.

Some tools offer sentiment indicators that quantify the overall sentiment of a particular cryptocurrency based on social media discussions. These indicators range from sentiment scores to sentiment indices, helping traders gauge whether the community sentiment is positive, negative, or neutral.

Visualizing sentiment through word clouds and emotion analytics adds a layer of insight to sentiment analysis. Word clouds display the most frequently used words and phrases within a corpus of text, providing a snapshot of the prevailing sentiments. Larger and bolder words indicate higher frequency.

Emotion analytics, an advanced form of sentiment analysis, delves into the emotional nuances expressed in text. Beyond positive and negative sentiment, emotion analytics identifies emotions including joy, anger, fear, and sadness. This deeper analysis provides a richer understanding of the emotional currents driving sentiment.

Event-driven sentiment analysis integrates news and event data to gauge sentiment shifts resulting from specific occurrences. News articles, press releases, and market updates can trigger pronounced changes in sentiment. By aligning sentiment data with news events, traders can decipher cause-and-effect relationships between sentiment and market reactions.

For instance, regulatory announcements, technological upgrades, or partnership agreements can trigger sharp shifts in sentiment. Traders can anticipate potential price movements by tracking sentiment spikes in proximity to such events.

Engaging with the cryptocurrency community and participating in discussions can offer traders first-hand insights into prevailing sentiment. Online forums like Reddit, dedicated cryptocurrency platforms, and social media channels allow traders to share opinions and engage in debates. Active participation will enable traders to gauge the community's mood and uncover sentiment trends.

However, community engagement requires critical thinking and discernment. Not all opinions and discussions accurately reflect the broader sentiment, as biased or manipulated information can sway discussions. Therefore, traders must approach community engagement with a balanced perspective.

While sentiment analysis tools and methods offer valuable insights, several challenges and considerations must be acknowledged. First, sentiment analysis does not provide absolute predictions of price movements. Market sentiment can be influenced by short-term emotions, rumors, or manipulation, leading to unexpected shifts.

Second, the cryptocurrency market is subject to extreme volatility. Rapid sentiment shifts can lead to abrupt price movements, and reliance solely on sentiment analysis without considering technical and fundamental factors can expose traders to risk.

Third, sentiment analysis tools must be carefully selected. Each tool employs unique algorithms and methodologies, which can lead to variations in sentiment scores. Traders must validate the accuracy and reliability of sentiment analysis platforms before making decisions based on their insights.

In conclusion, tools and methods for sentiment analysis in crypto trading provide a window into the emotional currents that drive price trends. The digital echo chamber of social media, online forums, and news platforms creates a dynamic environment where emotions reverberate and influence market sentiment.
Traders can unveil insights that guide their trading strategies by harnessing natural language processing, sentiment analysis platforms, social media tracking tools,

word clouds, emotion analytics, event-driven analysis, and community engagement. However, a balanced approach integrating sentiment analysis with technical and fundamental analysis is essential for making well-informed and prudent trading decisions.

Impact of social media and news on cryptocurrency prices

In the dynamic world of cryptocurrencies, where innovation and speculation intersect, the influence of social media and news on cryptocurrency prices has become a defining feature. The rise of digital communication platforms, coupled with the rapid dissemination of news, has created an ecosystem where information, opinions, and emotions circulate at lightning speed, shaping market sentiment and driving price movements. This section delves into the multifaceted impact of social media and news on cryptocurrency prices, exploring the mechanisms, dynamics, and challenges that underline this digital symbiosis.

The digital age has transformed how information is created, shared, and consumed. Social media platforms, including Telegram, Twitter, Reddit, and online cryptocurrency forums, have emerged as breeding grounds for discussions, debates, and analyses related to cryptocurrencies. These platforms facilitate the rapid exchange of opinions, news updates, and market insights, connecting traders, investors, enthusiasts, and experts in a global digital community.

Whether from traditional financial news outlets or dedicated cryptocurrency news platforms, news is also disseminated unprecedentedly. In an era of real-time updates, news articles, blog posts, and press releases can instantly impact the market sentiment surrounding cryptocurrencies.

Social media platforms are fertile ground for propagating sentiments that influence cryptocurrency prices. Traders and investors turn to platforms like Twitter, where influential figures, market analysts, and even high-profile individuals share their insights and opinions. A single tweet from a prominent individual can trigger cascading effects, leading to rapid price fluctuations.

Hashtags, trending topics, and discussions on social media can amplify sentiments, creating a sense of urgency that drives market participants to take action. Whether it's discussions about new technological developments, regulatory shifts, or market trends, social media platforms serve as a digital megaphone that magnifies sentiment-driven narratives.

News events, ranging from regulatory announcements to technological upgrades, possess the potential to trigger seismic shifts in cryptocurrency prices. Positive news, such as approving a cryptocurrency-related ETF or a significant partnership agreement, can inject optimism into the market and lead to price surges. Conversely, negative news, such as regulatory crackdowns or security breaches, can send shockwaves that lead to panic selling and price drops.

The phenomenon of news-driven price movements is heightened in cryptocurrency due to its relatively nascent nature and lack of established fundamentals. Cryptocurrencies often lack the traditional revenue models, earnings reports, and balance sheets that drive price movements in conventional financial markets. As a result, news events carry a disproportionate impact on cryptocurrency prices.

The viral nature of social media and the allure of quick profits contribute to the phenomenon of hype and FOMO (fear of missing out) in the cryptocurrency market. Trending discussions, celebrity endorsements, and speculative narratives can create waves of excitement and enthusiasm, spurring retail investors to jump on board with the hope of capitalizing on rapid price gains.

Hype-driven price movements, however, can also lead to market distortions and bubbles. The lack of fundamental value to justify price increases can result in overvaluation and subsequent price crashes. Traders must exercise caution and discernment when assessing hype-driven trends, distinguishing between sustainable growth and speculative euphoria.

While social media and news have revolutionized the information landscape, they also pose challenges and risks. One such challenge is spreading false information, rumors, and manipulated narratives. Without strict regulations, individuals and groups can exploit social media platforms to manipulate sentiment and induce price movements for personal gain.

The concept of "pump-and-dump" schemes exemplifies this manipulation. Orchestrators artificially inflate the price of a cryptocurrency through coordinated positive messaging on social media platforms, luring unsuspecting investors into buying at inflated prices. Once the price reaches a peak, the orchestrators sell their holdings, making the price to plummet and resulting in losses for those who bought in during the hype.

Given social media's and news's potent impact on cryptocurrency prices, traders and investors must adopt strategies that allow them to navigate this digital storm with insight and prudence.

First, critical thinking and verification are paramount. News and opinions should be cross-referenced with reliable sources, and claims should be scrutinized before influencing trading decisions.

Second, an understanding of market sentiment is essential. Traders should recognize that sentiment-driven price movements can be short-lived and influenced by emotions rather than underlying fundamentals.

Third, risk management becomes crucial. Given sentiment-driven price movements' rapid and unpredictable nature, setting stop-loss orders and diversifying portfolios can help mitigate potential losses.

Fourth, long-term fundamentals should be considered. While social media and news can create short-term volatility, understanding technological developments, adoption trends, and market positioning remains integral to making informed investment decisions.

In conclusion, the impact of social media and news on cryptocurrency prices highlights the digital age's profound influence on the financial landscape. The digital echo chamber of social media platforms and the instantaneous spread of news have magnified sentiment-driven narratives, creating an ecosystem where emotions, opinions, and news events interact to shape market sentiment and price trends.

Incorporating sentiment analysis into trading strategies

The cryptocurrency trading landscape is characterized by its volatility, innovation, and the unique interplay of technological advancements and market sentiment. As digital assets gain prominence, understanding the emotional currents that drive price movements has become essential to successful trading strategies. Sentiment analysis, a method of gauging market sentiment based on social media, news, and online discussions, has emerged as a potent tool for traders seeking to traverse the complex and rapidly evolving world of cryptocurrency trading. This section delves into the intricacies of incorporating sentiment analysis into crypto trading strategies, exploring its methodologies, benefits, challenges, and the symbiotic relationship between technology and emotions.

Sentiment analysis leverages advancements in natural language processing (NLP) and machine learning to decipher the emotional nuances embedded within the digital discourse of social media and news platforms. In an era where opinions and information circulate at unprecedented speeds, sentiment analysis provides traders with a lens through which they can peer into the emotional currents that drive price movements.

This fusion of technology and emotions has revolutionized trading strategies. By deciphering sentiment from text data, traders gain insights into prevailing market sentiment, which can influence decision-making, risk management, and the timing of trades. Incorporating sentiment analysis into crypto trading strategies empowers traders to navigate the intricate emotional landscape with a greater understanding of the market's mood.

Sentiment analysis employs diverse methodologies to assess market sentiment. Natural language processing algorithms analyze text data from social media posts, news articles, online forums, and regulatory announcements. These algorithms identify keywords, linguistic patterns, and context to classify sentiment as positive, negative, or neutral. Some advanced methodologies delve deeper, categorizing sentiment intensity and even specific emotions.

Sentiment analysis platforms aggregate data from various sources, transforming the qualitative language of emotions into quantitative sentiment scores. These scores provide traders with actionable insights, offering a snapshot of prevailing sentiment and potential market trends.

Incorporating sentiment analysis into crypto trading strategies offers a range of benefits that enhance decision-making and risk management.

First, sentiment analysis provides an additional layer of information that complements traditional technical and fundamental analysis. It can confirm or challenge existing trading hypotheses, validating price movements driven by sentiment trends.

Second, sentiment analysis offers an edge in volatile markets. Rapid price movements, often influenced by news or social media narratives, can be anticipated by monitoring sentiment trends. Traders can adjust their strategies based on shifting sentiment, mitigating potential losses or capitalizing on opportunities.

Third, sentiment analysis can uncover hidden patterns. By analyzing sentiment trends over time, traders can identify correlations between sentiment spikes and price movements, creating a predictive framework for future price changes.

Incorporating sentiment analysis into crypto trading strategies requires a nuanced approach acknowledging challenges and considerations.

First, sentiment analysis is not foolproof. The emotional nuances of human language can be complex and context-dependent, leading to misinterpretations by algorithms. False positives and false negatives in sentiment classifications can occur.

Second, sentiment analysis requires a balance between short-term trends and long-term fundamentals. Sentiment-driven price movements can be short-lived, and traders must exercise discernment to distinguish between sentiment-driven volatility and sustainable trends.

Third, sentiment analysis is susceptible to manipulation and misinformation. Traders must validate the credibility of news sources and remain aware of orchestrated sentiment campaigns designed to induce price movements for personal gain.

Incorporating sentiment analysis into crypto trading strategies involves integrating sentiment insights with technical and fundamental analyses.

First, traders should recognize that sentiment is a valuable supplementary tool rather than a sole basis for trading decisions. Combining sentiment analysis with technical indicators and chart patterns enhances the accuracy of predictions.

Second, sentiment analysis can inform the timing of trades. Traders may select to enter or exit positions based on sentiment-driven trends while considering support and resistance levels identified through technical analysis.

Third, sentiment analysis can guide risk management. Extreme sentiment shifts can be indicators of market tops or bottoms. Traders can set stop-loss orders or take profits based on sentiment-driven price movements.

While sentiment analysis provides insights into the emotional currents that drive price movements, traders must also embrace emotional discipline. Emotional reactions to sentiment trends can lead to impulsive decisions, contradicting a well-structured trading plan.

Traders should approach sentiment analysis with a balanced mindset. Recognizing that sentiment can shift rapidly, traders should avoid chasing short-term trends driven by emotions and instead make decisions aligned with their trading strategies and risk tolerance.

As the cryptocurrency market evolves, sentiment analysis will play an increasingly significant role in trading strategies. Traders who harness its power, exercise emotional discipline, and balance sentiment insights with sound trading principles are poised to thrive in the emotionally-driven future of trading, where emotions and technology synergize to define market trends.

CHAPTER VI

Market Trends and Patterns

Identifying and analyzing market trends

In the fast-paced and technologically-driven world of cryptocurrency trading, identifying and analyzing market trends is crucial for traders seeking to navigate the volatile and rapidly changing landscape. Unlike traditional financial markets, cryptocurrencies' nascent and digital nature adds complexity to trend identification. This section delves into the methodologies, tools, and insights that guide traders in identifying and analyzing market trends in crypto trading, exploring the distinctive characteristics, challenges, and strategies that define this unique market ecosystem.

Cryptocurrencies, digital assets powered by blockchain technology, have revolutionized the financial landscape. Unlike traditional markets, cryptocurrencies trade 24/7 across global exchanges, making price movements continuous and relentless. The absence of centralized regulation and the prevalence of retail participation contribute to heightened volatility, creating opportunities and challenges for traders.

Technical analysis, a cornerstone of trend identification, is equally vital in cryptocurrency. Price charts, candlestick patterns, and technical indicators empower traders to decode market sentiment and forecast future price movements. Chart patterns such as ascending triangles, head and shoulders, and double bottoms offer insights into potential trend reversals or continuations.

Moving averages, Relative Strength Index (RSI), and Moving Average Convergence Divergence (MACD) are essential technical tools. Moving averages smooth price fluctuations, aiding in trend identification. RSI and MACD gauge overbought and oversold conditions and momentum shifts.

Cryptocurrencies are renowned for their extreme price volatility, driven by sentiment shifts, regulatory news, technological developments, and macroeconomic factors. This volatility amplifies the importance of identifying trends accurately. By examining posts on social media, articles on the news, and online forums, sentiment analysis, which is supported by natural language processing (NLP), evaluates market sentiment. Positive sentiment can drive price surges, while negative sentiment can trigger sell-offs. Incorporating sentiment insights into trend analysis provides a holistic view of market dynamics.

Support and resistance levels, vital in trend identification, exhibit unique behavior in the cryptocurrency realm. These levels often reflect psychological milestones and historical price points. Breakouts from these levels can signal trend changes. Cryptocurrencies are known for their propensity to exhibit sharp price movements near support and resistance levels, often called "whipsaws." Traders must exercise caution and verify breakout signals to avoid false trends caused by market manipulation.

Timeframes play a significant role in crypto trend analysis. Short-term traders focus on intraday or short-term trends, while swing traders and long-term investors assess trends on higher timeframes. Longer timeframes, such as daily or weekly, provide a clearer picture of the prevailing trend direction. Timeframe selection depends on trading goals, risk tolerance, and market conditions. Crypto traders must align their strategies with the chosen timeframe and consider multiple timeframes for a comprehensive view.

Cryptocurrencies often exhibit correlations with each other and with traditional financial markets. Identifying these correlations can aid in trend analysis. For example, if Bitcoin (usually considered a bellwether) exhibits a particular trend, it may influence other cryptocurrencies. Macro trends, such as adoption rates, regulatory developments, and technological upgrades, also impact cryptocurrency trends. Positive regulatory news can trigger bullish trends, while security breaches or negative adoption trends can lead to bearish sentiment.

While the methodologies for identifying and analyzing trends apply broadly, cryptocurrency trading presents unique challenges. The absence of historical data compared to traditional markets can make trend analysis more challenging. Rapid price movements and thin order books can result in slippage and unexpected trend reversals. Moreover, cryptocurrency markets are susceptible to market manipulation due to lower liquidity and the absence of regulatory oversight. Traders must be cautious and verify trend signals with multiple indicators and data sources.

To overcome these challenges, traders adopt holistic strategies that integrate technical analysis, sentiment analysis, and fundamental research.

Technical analysis, combined with cryptocurrency-specific indicators like the Crypto Fear and Greed Index or on-chain data, provides a comprehensive view. Sentiment analysis platforms aggregate social media sentiment scores, offering insights into prevailing market sentiment.

Fundamental research delves into technological advancements, partnerships, adoption rates, and regulatory developments. Fundamental analysis can enhance trend identification accuracy when paired with technical and sentiment analyses.

Risk management remains paramount in crypto trend trading due to the market's inherent volatility. Traders should set stop-loss orders, diversify portfolios, and avoid overexposing themselves to a single asset. Position sizing should be aligned with risk tolerance, considering potential price swings. Traders must also remain vigilant for unexpected news events that could trigger trend reversals.

In conclusion, identifying and analyzing market trends in crypto trading requires a multifaceted approach that combines technical analysis, sentiment insights, and fundamental understanding. The unique characteristics of the cryptocurrency landscape, such as continuous trading, extreme volatility, and sentiment-driven movements, amplify the importance of accurate trend identification.

Bull and bear markets: characteristics and indicators

In cryptocurrency trading, the rhythms of bull and bear markets define the ebb and flow of investor sentiment, shaping price trajectories and influencing trading strategies. These two distinct market phases encapsulate the emotional currents that drive the cryptocurrency landscape, marked by periods of exuberant optimism and cautious pessimism. This section delves into the characteristics and indicators defining bull and bear markets in the context of crypto trading, exploring the digital nuances, challenges, and strategic considerations traders must navigate in this innovative and volatile arena.

A bull market in crypto trading is characterized by an extended period of rising asset prices and a prevailing sense of optimism and investor enthusiasm. During a bull market, prices of cryptocurrencies experience significant appreciation, often driven by technological advancements, positive news events, and growing adoption. One of the defining characteristics of a crypto bull market is the influx of retail and institutional investors seeking to capitalize on the upward momentum. Market sentiment becomes euphoric, and phrases like "To the moon!" symbolize the optimistic outlook. The rapid increase in trading volumes and the proliferation of initial coin offerings (ICOs) are typical hallmarks of a bull market.

Conversely, a bear market in crypto trading ushers in declining asset prices and dampens sentiment. During a bear market, investor confidence wanes, leading to heightened caution and risk aversion levels. Adverse news events, regulatory uncertainties, or security breaches often contribute to the negative sentiment. Bear markets in crypto trading are characterized by prolonged periods of price decline and increased market volatility. Investors who were once fervently optimistic may experience "panic selling," as fear of further losses takes hold. Trading volumes may decrease, and market activity often becomes subdued.

Cryptocurrency traders rely on various indicators to identify and distinguish between bull and bear markets. One key indicator is the prolonged direction of price movement. In a bull market, asset prices consistently trend upwards over an extended period, while in a bear market, prices exhibit a sustained downtrend. Technical indicators play a crucial role in confirming these trends. Moving averages, which smooth out price fluctuations, can signal the onset of a bull market when shorter-term moving averages cross above longer-term moving averages. Conversely, a cross below may indicate the beginning of a bear market.

Sentiment analysis holds particular significance in cryptocurrency, where emotions and news events can drive extreme price volatility. Cryptocurrency traders often monitor social media platforms, online forums, and news outlets to gauge prevailing sentiment. Positive sentiment can fuel bullish trends, while negative sentiment can contribute to bearish spirals. However, sentiment analysis in crypto trading presents unique challenges. The cryptocurrency market's relatively young and rapidly evolving nature can result in excessive price volatility and sentiment-driven price swings. Traders must exercise caution when relying solely on sentiment analysis and consider other technical and fundamental factors.

Transitions between bull and bear markets are rarely instantaneous, often marked by periods of consolidation, corrections, or sideways movements. These transitional phases can be challenging to navigate, as price volatility may decrease and market sentiment becomes uncertain. Cryptocurrency traders must be prepared to identify signals that indicate the potential end of a bear market or the emergence of a new bull market. False breakouts, where prices temporarily break through resistance levels before retracing, can complicate trend identification.

Traders in cryptocurrency use diverse strategies to navigate both bull and bear markets.

During a bull market, trend-following strategies are widespread. Traders attempt to capitalize on the upward momentum by entering positions aligned with the prevailing trend. Techniques such as buying on pullbacks or breakouts can be effective, provided risk management practices are in place.

In a bear market, traders often adopt short-selling strategies or consider alternative investments that can profit from price declines. Hedging techniques, such as using derivatives or inverse ETFs, provide avenues to mitigate potential losses.

In conclusion, bull and bear markets in crypto trading represent the digital symphony of optimism and pessimism that shapes the landscape of cryptocurrencies. While characterized by distinct characteristics and indicators, these market phases are deeply influenced by sentiment, technological advancements, and news events unique to the digital age.

Recognizing common market patterns (head and shoulders, cup and handle, etc.)

In the intricate world of cryptocurrency trading, where price movements often resemble a complex dance, recognizing common market patterns is a skill that sets astute traders apart. These visual formations, such as head and shoulders, cup and handle, and triangles, offer valuable insights into potential trend reversals, continuations, and price targets. This section delves into the significance of recognizing common market patterns in crypto trading, exploring the characteristics, interpretations, and strategic considerations that empower traders to navigate the digital landscape with precision and foresight.

Market patterns represent supply and demand dynamics, investor sentiment, and the interplay between buyers and sellers. These patterns form due to market participants' reactions to news, events, and evolving trends. By identifying and understanding these patterns, traders can anticipate potential price movements and align their strategies accordingly.

The head and shoulders pattern is a classic reversal pattern that signals a potential trend shift. It is comprised of three peaks: a higher peak (the head) flanked by two lower peaks (the shoulders). When the price breaks below the neckline—a line that connects the lows of the troughs—the pattern is completed. A head and shoulders pattern signifies the transition from a bullish trend to a bearish one. The first shoulder represents initial resistance, the head marks a higher peak and a strong reversal signal, and the second shoulder signifies diminishing bullish momentum. The neckline breach validates the pattern, indicating that bearish sentiment has gained dominance.

A continuation pattern that frequently appears during bullish trends is the cup and handle pattern. It resembles the shape of a teacup or coffee cup, followed by a smaller consolidation known as the handle. This pattern signifies a brief period of consolidation before the bullish trend resumes. The cup and handle pattern reflects a temporary pullback followed by renewed buying interest. Traders often interpret this pattern as an opportunity to enter positions, anticipating an upward trend continuation. The handle's lower volume indicates decreased selling pressure and sets the stage for the next upward move.

Triangles are characterized by converging trendlines representing a decreasing period of price volatility. There are three main types: ascending, descending, and symmetrical triangles. Ascending triangles indicate potential bullish breakouts, descending triangles suggest bearish breakouts, and symmetrical triangles signify a possible continuation of the existing trend. Triangles represent a balance between buying and selling pressure, culminating in a breakout that often leads to significant price movement. Traders closely monitor the triangle's apex, where the trendlines converge, as it often precedes a breakout or breakdown.

Rectangles denote periods of consolidation and indicate a temporary pause in the prevailing trend. They are formed when prices oscillate within horizontal support and resistance levels. Rectangles can be continuation or reversal patterns, depending on the preceding trend. The rectangle's breakout or breakdown signifies the potential resumption of the prior trend. Traders consider the rectangle's height as a target for the price movement following the breakout.

Recognizing common market patterns in crypto trading is a skill that requires a keen eye, technical acumen, and a thorough understanding of market dynamics. Traders must be cautious of false signals, which can occur due to market manipulation, unexpected news events, or irregular price behavior. Integration with other technical and fundamental analysis tools enhances pattern recognition accuracy. Traders often use technical indicators, moving averages, and volume analysis to validate pattern formations and anticipate potential breakouts.

In conclusion, recognizing common market patterns in crypto trading is akin to deciphering a visual mosaic that unveils the intricate interplay of market forces and investor sentiment. These patterns give traders a glimpse into potential future price movements, offering a foundation for informed decision-making and strategic planning.

Using trend analysis for entry and exit points

In the fast-paced and exhilarating realm of cryptocurrency trading, mastering the art of trend analysis is a foundational skill that separates successful traders from the rest. Trend analysis empowers traders to precisely identify potential entry and exit points, enabling them to ride the waves of price movements and capitalize on profitable opportunities. This section delves into the significance of using trend analysis for entry and exit points in crypto trading, exploring the methodologies, strategies, and considerations that guide traders in navigating the dynamic and ever-evolving landscape of digital assets.

Trend analysis is a trader's compass in the complex and often unpredictable cryptocurrency market. At its core, trend analysis involves studying price charts, identifying patterns, and interpreting technical indicators to decipher the prevailing trend direction. This analytical approach enables traders to make informed decisions based on past and present price behavior, offering insights into potential future price movements.

Identifying optimal entry points is essential for traders seeking to maximize potential gains while minimizing risks. Trend analysis is pivotal in pinpointing entry points that align with the prevailing trend direction. Traders often employ various technical tools to identify entry points. For instance, in an uptrend, traders may look for pullbacks or retracements to enter a position at a more favorable price. Fibonacci retracement levels, derived from the Fibonacci sequence, help traders identify potential support levels during retracements. Breakouts from chart patterns, such as ascending triangles or bullish flag formations, also signal possible entry points. A breakout occurs when prices breach a pattern's resistance, indicating a potential trend continuation.

Equally crucial to successful trading is identifying appropriate exit points. Effective exit strategies allow traders to lock in profits and protect against potential losses. Trend analysis aids in determining exit points that align with trend reversals or potential price exhaustion. Traders typically employ technical indicators like the Moving Average Convergence Divergence and Relative Strength Index to spot overbought and oversold conditions. When these indicators suggest that an asset is reaching extreme levels, it may be an indication to consider exiting a position. Trailing stop-loss orders are another technique used to secure profits while allowing for potential further gains. As the price moves in the trader's favor, the stop-loss order is adjusted to trail the price, preserving profits if the trend reverses.

While trend analysis offers valuable insights, successful application requires careful consideration of various factors.

First, traders must select appropriate timeframes for analysis. Short-term traders may focus on intraday trends, while longer-term investors consider daily or weekly trends. Aligning timeframes with trading goals is essential to accurate analysis.

Second, confirmation is key. Traders should never rely solely on one indicator or pattern. Combining multiple indicators, such as moving averages alongside momentum oscillators, enhances the accuracy of trend analysis.

Third, risk management remains paramount. Entering a position based on trend analysis is not a guarantee of success. Reduced exposure to market volatility is achieved by diversifying the portfolio among several assets and setting stop-loss orders which limit potential losses.

Traders employ various strategies that leverage trend analysis for entry and exit points. Trend-following strategies involve entering positions in the direction of the prevailing trend. Techniques such as the Moving Average Crossover strategy use moving averages to signal potential entry and exit points. Counter-trend strategies, on the other hand, seek to capitalize on short-term reversals within a more significant trend. These strategies require a deep understanding of market psychology and may involve more risk.

In conclusion, using trend analysis for entry and exit points in crypto trading is an art that combines technical acumen, strategic thinking, and risk management. Traders who master trend analysis gain the ability to identify probable entry and exit points with precision, enhancing their chances of capitalizing on price movements and achieving profitable outcomes.

CHAPTER VII

Trading Strategies

Day trading, swing trading, and long-term investing

In the dynamic and rapidly evolving realm of cryptocurrency trading, the choice of trading strategy is paramount to achieving success and managing risk. Traders and investors navigate the digital landscape using distinct approaches tailored to different timeframes and market conditions. This section delves into the nuances and strategies of day trading, swing trading, as well as long-term investing in crypto trading, exploring the characteristics, benefits, and considerations that shape traders' decisions and determine their path to profitability.

Day trading is an active strategy that involves executing multiple trades within a single day, capitalizing on short-term price movements. Day traders seek to profit from volatility and exploit intraday trends by entering and exiting positions quickly.

The hallmark of day trading is its agility. Traders leverage technical analysis, chart patterns, and technical indicators to identify potential price movements within short timeframes. Strategies include scalping, where traders make numerous small trades throughout the day, and momentum trading, where they capitalize on sudden price surges.

While day trading offers the potential for quick profits, it requires immense discipline, focus, and the ability to manage risk effectively. Traders must stay updated on news events, monitor real-time price movements, and make split-second decisions.

Swing trading balances the intensity of day trading and the patience of long-term investing. Swing traders seek to capture price movements that span a few days to several weeks, capitalizing on mid-term trends.

Technical analysis is utilized by swing traders to spot future price trend reversals or continuations. They often use chart patterns, moving averages, and trendlines to make informed decisions. The goal is to catch the "swing" of a trend as prices move from one extreme to another.

Swing trading allows more flexibility than day trading, as traders have more time to analyze market conditions and make decisions. However, it still demands diligence in monitoring price movements and adapting to changing market dynamics.

Long-term investing involves holding positions for extended periods, often months or years, to capitalize on significant price appreciation over time. Long-term investors are less concerned with short-term price fluctuations and more focused on the asset's potential.

Long-term investing aligns with the "HODL" mentality prevalent in the crypto community, emphasizing the belief in the long-term potential of an asset. This strategy is suited for those who have confidence in cryptocurrency technology, adoption, and fundamentals.

While long-term investing reduces the need for constant monitoring, it requires patience and a strong conviction in the chosen assets. Investors must conduct thorough research, consider project development and adoption factors, and have the emotional fortitude to withstand market downturns.

Day trading, swing trading, and long-term investing offer distinct benefits and considerations.

Day trading provides the potential for quick profits, allowing traders to take advantage of intraday volatility. However, it demands intense focus, rapid decision-making, and disciplined risk management. The constant need to monitor the markets can be mentally and emotionally taxing.

Swing trading gives traders more flexibility and the opportunity to capture mid-term trends. Traders have more time to analyze patterns and make informed decisions. However, swing trading still requires vigilance and adapting to changing market conditions.

Long-term investing is well-suited for individuals who believe in the long-term potential of specific cryptocurrencies. It reduces the stress of constant monitoring and allows investors to ride out short-term price fluctuations. However, long-term investing requires patience, research, and the ability to withstand market volatility.

Choosing the right strategy in crypto trading depends on individual goals, risk tolerance, time commitment, and trading experience.

Novice traders often find day trading and swing trading challenging due to their intense nature and the need for technical expertise. Long-term investing might be more suitable for those seeking a more passive approach, focusing on the potential of the technology and its future impact.

Experienced traders may gravitate towards day or swing trading, leveraging their skills to capitalize on short- to mid-term price movements. These strategies require a deeper understanding of technical analysis, market trends, and risk management.

In conclusion, day trading, swing trading, and long-term investing offer different timeframes of opportunity in the vibrant world of crypto trading. Each strategy carries its benefits and challenges, catering to traders and investors with varying goals and preferences.

Scalping techniques for short-term gains

In the fast-paced and adrenaline-filled world of cryptocurrency trading, where price movements can change in the blink of an eye, scalping techniques have emerged as a favored strategy for traders seeking quick and frequent gains. Scalping, a short-term trading method, involves executing multiple trades within a single day to profit from small price differentials. This section delves into the intricacies of scalping techniques in crypto trading, exploring the strategies, considerations, and challenges traders face in navigating this lightning-fast landscape to secure short-term gains.

Scalping is rooted in the principle of capitalizing on minor price fluctuations, aiming to profit from small price changes that occur within minutes or seconds. Scalpers target assets with high liquidity and tight spreads, enabling them to enter and exit positions swiftly without incurring significant transaction costs. One of the critical advantages of scalping is its ability to generate multiple opportunities in a single trading day. While each trade may yield a small profit, the cumulative gains can be substantial over time.

Technical analysis is the bedrock of scalping strategies. Scalpers rely on a combination of technical indicators, chart patterns, and short-term moving averages to make rapid trading decisions. Moving averages, such as the 5-period or 10-period moving average, provide insights into short-term price trends. Scalpers look for crossovers or changes in slope to signal potential entry and exit points. Chart patterns, such as flags, pennants, and triangles, offer valuable insights into potential short-term price movements. Scalpers also use oscillators like the Relative Strength Index (RSI) to gauge overbought and oversold conditions, assisting in timing their trades.

While scalping offers the allure of quick gains, it comes with its own set of considerations and challenges. First, scalpers must have access to a reliable and fast execution platform. Latency can lead to missed opportunities or unfavorable price entries. Scalpers often prefer direct market access (DMA) platforms for their speed and efficiency.

Second, risk management is paramount. Due to the frequent trading nature of scalping, a single losing trade can quickly erase accumulated gains. Scalpers use tight stop-loss orders to limit potential losses and position sizing techniques to manage risk.

Third, emotional discipline is essential. The fast-paced nature of scalping can lead to stress and decision-making pressure. Traders must maintain a cool head and adhere to their predefined strategies.

Scalping techniques are typically employed on short timeframes, ranging from seconds to minutes. Scalpers monitor order books, level II data, and real-time price movements to make rapid trading decisions. Market conditions also play a role in the success of scalping strategies. High volatility and liquidity are conducive to scalping, creating opportunities for quick price movements. News events and sudden market shifts can significantly impact scalping outcomes, as volatility can lead to both gains and losses.

Scalping techniques can vary in approach. Tape reading, for example, involves closely monitoring real-time market data to identify patterns that indicate potential price movements. Time and sales data, bid-ask spreads, and order book dynamics are analyzed to make quick decisions. Another form of scalping is called "market making," in which traders place limit orders on each side of the market to create liquidity. This strategy aims to profit from the bid-ask spread and requires a deep understanding of market dynamics.

The psychology of scalping is unique, as traders must be comfortable with rapid decision-making and accepting small profits. Scalpers are more concerned with the frequency of winning trades rather than the magnitude of each profit. The pressure of making quick decisions and the potential for rapid losses can lead to emotional stress. Scalpers must develop psychological resilience, maintain discipline, and adhere to their strategies despite market fluctuations.

In conclusion, scalping techniques for short-term gains in crypto trading offer a dynamic and fast-paced approach to profiting from small price differentials. This strategy requires technical acumen, rapid decision-making, risk management, and emotional discipline.

While scalping has the potential to produce quick gains, there are drawbacks as well. Traders must be equipped with reliable execution platforms, adhere to risk management protocols, and manage psychological pressures.

Scalping variations, such as tape reading and market making, provide traders diverse approaches to capitalize on short-term price movements.

In the ever-evolving and exhilarating realm of crypto trading, scalping is a strategy that demands precision, agility, and a deep understanding of market dynamics. By mastering the art of scalping techniques, traders navigate the lightning-fast terrain with insight, strategy, and the potential for short-term gains in the whirlwind of cryptocurrency price movements.

Momentum trading and contrarian strategies

In the ever-evolving landscape of cryptocurrency trading, strategies that harness the power of momentum and contrarian trading have emerged as prominent approaches to capitalize on market trends and sentiment shifts. Momentum trading involves riding the waves of established trends, while contrarian strategies seek to profit from trend reversals. This section delves into the intricacies of momentum trading and contrarian strategies in crypto trading, exploring the methodologies, benefits, and considerations that guide traders navigating the waters of market sentiment and price movements.

Momentum trading revolves around the principle that assets tend to stay in motion. Traders who employ momentum strategies seek to capitalize on existing trends, entering positions that align with the prevailing momentum. This strategy is especially effective during periods of strong market trends and is often used by traders seeking short- to mid-term gains.

Technical indicators play a crucial role in momentum trading. Moving averages, Relative Strength Index (RSI), and MACD are frequently used to identify trends and gauge the strength of momentum. Traders look for crossovers, overbought or oversold conditions, and changes in slope to signal potential entry and exit points.

Momentum traders often use breakout strategies, where they enter positions when prices breach resistance levels. Pullbacks or retracements are also monitored for potential entry opportunities, allowing traders to buy during short-term dips within an overarching bullish trend.

Momentum trading offers several benefits, including the potential for capturing significant price movements during strong trends. It enables traders to profit from the excitement of rising prices and ride the wave of market sentiment. Additionally, momentum strategies are relatively straightforward to implement, making them accessible to traders of varying experience levels.

However, momentum trading is not without challenges. False breakouts or sudden reversals can lead to losses, especially if traders fail to accurately identify a trend's strength. Additionally, overextended trends may result in overbought or oversold conditions, increasing the risk of a market correction.

Contrarian strategies, in contrast to momentum trading, involve going against the prevailing market sentiment. Contrarian traders believe that market participants' emotions often lead to overreactions, creating opportunities when the market sentiment diverges from the fundamentals.

One popular contrarian approach is mean reversion trading, where traders anticipate that prices will revert to their historical average after deviating significantly. This strategy involves buying during downtrends and selling during uptrends. The idea is that extreme price movements are temporary and that assets will eventually return to their intrinsic value.

Technical indicators, such as Bollinger Bands, can aid contrarian traders in identifying potential reversal points. Oversold conditions or price divergences from indicators can signal that a trend may be due for a reversal. Contrarian strategies allow traders to enter positions at favorable prices, especially when market sentiment has swung to an extreme. By capitalizing on market overreactions, contrarian traders have the potential to achieve profitable outcomes.

However, contrarian strategies come with their own set of challenges. Timing is critical, as entering a position prematurely during a potential trend reversal can result in losses. Market sentiment can persist longer than expected, leading to further price declines or surges, and contrarian traders must be prepared to weather short-term fluctuations.

Effective traders often integrate elements of both momentum and contrarian strategies to strike a balance between capitalizing on existing trends and profiting from sentiment shifts.

One approach is to use momentum to confirm the direction of a trade before executing a contrarian strategy. For example, a contrarian trader may wait for signs of a trend reversal, such as divergence in indicators or oversold conditions, before entering a position that aligns with the reversal direction.

Another strategy involves using momentum to guide the timing of a contrarian trade. A trader may wait for signs of trend exhaustion or weakening momentum before executing a contrarian strategy to capitalize on the potential shift.

In conclusion, momentum trading and contrarian strategies are two distinct approaches that allow traders to navigate the ever-shifting currents of market sentiment and price movements in the cryptocurrency trading landscape. Momentum traders ride the waves of established trends, relying on technical indicators and breakout strategies to capture short- to mid-term gains. Contrarian traders, on the other hand, profit from sentiment shifts by going against the prevailing market sentiment, often using mean reversion and timing indicators to identify potential reversal points.

Both strategies have their benefits and challenges, and successful traders often integrate elements of both approaches to strike a balance between capturing trend momentum and profiting from sentiment-driven shifts. By harnessing the power of momentum and contrarian strategies, traders navigate the complex terrain of cryptocurrency trading with insight, strategy, and a deeper understanding of the nuanced interplay between market sentiment and price movements.

Diversification and portfolio management

In cryptocurrency trading, where volatility and unpredictability reign, diversification and effective portfolio management emerge as a strategic imperative for traders and investors. As the crypto market fluctuates with enthusiasm, the principles of diversification offer a shield against excessive risk, while astute portfolio management guides the allocation of resources for optimal outcomes. This section delves into the intricacies of diversification and portfolio management in crypto trading, exploring the methodologies, advantages, and considerations that shape resilient and balanced investment approaches.

Diversification, often heralded as the cornerstone of successful investing, involves spreading investments across different assets to mitigate risk. In the volatile realm of cryptocurrencies, diversification serves as a protective mechanism against the potential downfall of a single asset.

Diversification can take various forms. Traders may diversify across different cryptocurrencies, asset classes (such as utility tokens, stablecoins, and security tokens), industries, or geographical regions. By holding a mix of assets that respond differently to market conditions, traders reduce their exposure to any single asset's price volatility.

The critical advantage of diversification is the potential to achieve stable returns and cushion the impact of sudden market shifts. While diversification cannot eliminate all risks, it significantly reduces the likelihood of a catastrophic loss.

Effective portfolio management involves allocating resources strategically to balance risk and reward. When crafting a portfolio management strategy, traders and investors must consider their risk tolerance, investment goals, and time horizon.

One common approach to portfolio management is the Modern Portfolio Theory (MPT), which aims to optimize portfolio returns for a given level of risk. MPT involves creating a portfolio with a mix of assets that offers the highest expected return for a specific level of risk tolerance.

A key element of portfolio management is asset allocation. It involves deciding how much of the portfolio should be allocated to different asset classes. A balanced approach might combine high-risk, high-reward assets with more stable, low-risk ones.

Diversification and portfolio management offer numerous benefits for crypto traders and investors.

First, they help manage risk. A well-diversified portfolio is less susceptible to the drastic price swings in the crypto market. While some assets may experience losses, others may still perform well, providing stability.

Second, they promote consistent returns. By investing in various assets, traders can balance out the ups and downs of individual assets, resulting in more predictable overall returns.

Third, they cater to different investment goals. Traders with varying levels of risk tolerance and time horizons can adjust their portfolios to meet their particular objectives, whether they are looking for short-term profits, long-term growth, or a combination of both.

While diversification and portfolio management offer numerous benefits, there are also considerations and challenges to navigate.

Overdiversification, where a portfolio becomes so diversified that potential gains are diluted, can be counterproductive. Additionally, some assets may be highly correlated, reducing the benefits of diversification.

Market conditions and technological advancements can also impact portfolio performance. Traders must stay informed about market trends, regulatory changes, and emerging technologies that could affect the value of their assets.

Rebalancing is an essential aspect of portfolio management. Over time, asset values may shift, altering the original allocation. Regular rebalancing involves selling overperforming assets and buying underperforming ones to maintain the desired allocation.

Additionally important is adaptive management, which enables traders to modify their portfolios in response to shifting market conditions. If certain assets become obsolete or face regulatory challenges, traders may need to reallocate resources to more promising opportunities.

In conclusion, diversification and portfolio management are indispensable tools in the toolkit of successful crypto traders and investors. Diversification shields against concentrated risk, reducing vulnerability to the wild swings of the crypto market. Effective portfolio management, guided by sound allocation principles, aligns investment strategies with individual risk tolerance and objectives.

While diversification offers stability and risk mitigation, effective portfolio management ensures that resources are strategically allocated to achieve optimal outcomes. By considering asset allocation, risk tolerance, and investment goals, traders navigate the volatile waters of cryptocurrency trading with resilience, balance, and the potential for sustained growth.

In the dynamic and rapidly evolving world of cryptocurrencies, where the only constant is change, diversification and portfolio management are pillars of stability and strategic foresight. By crafting resilient investment approaches, traders and investors position themselves to weather market turbulence, seize opportunities, and pave the way for sustainable success in the captivating realm of crypto trading.

CHAPTER VIII

Risk Management and Capital Allocation

Importance of risk management in cryptocurrency trading

The need of risk management cannot be overstated in the thrilling world of cryptocurrency trading, where fortunes can be made and lost in the span of a single second. As traders navigate digital assets' dynamic and often unpredictable waters, managing risk effectively is a critical differentiator between success and failure. This section delves into the importance of risk management in cryptocurrency trading, exploring the methodologies, strategies, and considerations that guide traders in safeguarding their capital and optimizing their trading outcomes.

Risk in cryptocurrency trading arises from the inherent volatility of digital assets. Unlike traditional financial markets, the crypto landscape is characterized by rapid price fluctuations that news events, regulatory developments, technological shifts, and market sentiment can trigger. While volatility presents opportunities for substantial gains, it also exposes traders to the potential for significant losses.

Managing risk involves identifying, assessing, and mitigating potential threats to capital. The goal is not to eliminate risk entirely but rather to navigate it prudently and strategically to protect one's investment.

Various risk management methodologies have emerged to guide traders in pursuing capital preservation and profitable outcomes. One widely used approach is the concept of position sizing. This involves determining the amount of capital to allocate to a single trade based on risk tolerance, account size, and the potential loss on the trade. By adhering to a predetermined position size, traders can limit the impact of a single losing trade on their overall portfolio.

Another technique is setting stop-loss orders, which is an instruction to automatically sell an asset if its price reaches a certain level. This prevents losses from accumulating beyond a predefined threshold. Traders may choose different stop-loss levels based on their analysis of support and resistance levels, technical indicators, and market conditions.

Diversification, as previously discussed, is a robust risk management tool. By spreading investments across different assets, traders reduce their exposure to the price volatility of any single asset. Diversification can be acquired by investing in multiple cryptocurrencies, different asset classes, or even traditional financial instruments.

The goal of diversification is to develop a portfolio that is less susceptible to catastrophic losses. While some assets may decline in value, others may appreciate, providing stability to the overall portfolio.

Effective risk management includes considering the risk-to-reward ratio for each trade. This ratio assesses the potential profit of a trade compared to the possible loss.

A favorable risk-to-reward ratio indicates that the potential reward is greater than the potential loss, making the trade more attractive.

Traders often apply trade management techniques to optimize their risk-to-reward ratios. Techniques such as trailing stop-loss orders, where the stop-loss level adjusts as the trade moves in the trader's favor, can help secure profits while allowing for potential further gains.

The psychological aspect of risk management cannot be overlooked. Emotional discipline is essential for adhering to risk management strategies during market turbulence. Fear as well as greed can cloud judgment and lead traders to make impulsive decisions that deviate from their predetermined risk management plans.

Effective risk management requires emotional resilience and staying true to one's strategy even when faced with market uncertainty. Traders need to be prepared to accept losses as an inherent part of trading and not let fear dictate their actions.

Cryptocurrency trading is not immune to external risks, such as regulatory changes, security breaches, and market manipulation. Effective risk management extends beyond individual trades to encompass these broader risks.

Traders must stay informed about regulatory developments in different jurisdictions and adapt their strategies accordingly. Strong security measures, such as using secure wallets and two-factor authentication, helps safeguard against potential security breaches. Additionally, trading on reputable and regulated exchanges reduces the risk of falling victim to market manipulation.

In conclusion, the importance of risk management in cryptocurrency trading cannot be overstated. Effective risk management is a pillar of success in a market characterized by volatility, uncertainty, and rapid price movements. Traders who master risk management techniques, such as position sizing, setting stop-loss orders, and diversification, are better equipped to protect their capital, optimize their risk-to-reward ratios, and navigate the challenges of the crypto landscape.

Moreover, risk management is not merely a technical aspect of trading; it is deeply intertwined with psychology and discipline. Managing emotions, adhering to predetermined strategies, and staying resilient in the face of market fluctuations is crucial for successful risk management.

As traders venture into the captivating realm of cryptocurrency trading, they do so knowing that effective risk management is their ally, guiding them through the unpredictable and often exhilarating journey of digital asset investment. By safeguarding their capital and making informed decisions, traders position themselves for sustainable success in cryptocurrency trading.

Setting stop-loss and take-profit levels

In the high-stakes arena of cryptocurrency trading, where price movements can be as swift as they are unpredictable, setting stop-loss and take-profit levels emerges as a pivotal strategy for traders seeking to optimize their trading outcomes. These levels are gatekeepers, guiding traders to secure profits and limit losses. This section delves into the intricacies of setting stop-loss and take-profit levels in cryptocurrency trading, exploring the methodologies, considerations, and benefits that shape this crucial aspect of risk management and profit maximization.

Stop-loss and take-profit levels are pre-defined price points traders set to automatically execute specific actions when reached. Stop-loss orders limit potential losses by automatically selling an asset if its price falls to a specified level. On the other hand, take-profit orders are used to secure profits by automatically selling an asset when its price reaches a desired level of gain.

These levels are integral to a trader's risk management and profit-taking strategies. They enable traders to remove emotion from their decision-making process and ensure that trading actions align with their predetermined plans.

Setting appropriate stop-loss levels is a cornerstone of effective risk management. A stop-loss level is typically determined by assessing an acceptable percentage of loss relative to the trading capital. Traders often use technical analysis to identify support levels or key chart patterns that could indicate a potential trend reversal.

For example, if a trader has a risk tolerance of 2% per trade and is trading with a capital of $10,000, the stop-loss level would be set to trigger if the price moves against the trader by 2% of $10,000, resulting in a loss of $200.

Setting stop-loss levels too close to the entry price can lead to premature triggering due to market noise while setting them too far away can expose traders to excessive losses. Striking the right balance requires a combination of technical analysis, risk assessment, and an understanding of market dynamics.

Take-profit levels enable traders to lock in profits when the price reaches a predetermined target. Traders often use technical indicators, chart patterns, and historical price data to identify potential resistance levels or areas of profit-taking.

When setting take-profit levels, traders consider their profit targets, risk-to-reward ratios, and the potential for price movements. For instance, a trader with a risk-to-reward ratio of 1:2 may set a take-profit level at twice the distance of their stop-loss level, aiming to achieve a favorable risk-reward balance.

It's important to note that while take-profit levels secure profits, they can also prevent traders from fully capitalizing on extended price movements. Traders must balance securing profits and allowing for potential additional gains.

Setting stop-loss and take-profit levels requires a combination of technical analysis, risk assessment, and market understanding. However, traders must also consider external factors that can impact price movements.

News events, regulatory announcements, and sudden market shifts can trigger price movements that bypass pre-defined levels. Traders must stay informed about trade developments and be prepared to adapt their strategies accordingly.

Market volatility also poses challenges, as prices can experience rapid fluctuations that trigger stop-loss or take-profit orders before traders can react. Using wider stop-loss and take-profit ranges during periods of high volatility can mitigate this risk.

Various strategies are employed for setting stop-loss and take-profit levels, each tailored to a trader's risk tolerance, trading style, and objectives.

A conservative approach involves setting wider stop-loss and take-profit levels to allow for price fluctuations and reduce the risk of premature triggering. This approach is suited for traders with a lower risk tolerance who are willing to sacrifice some potential gains for greater capital preservation.

An aggressive approach involves setting tighter stop-loss and take-profit levels to maximize potential gains. This approach is suitable for traders seeking to capitalize on short-term price movements and who are comfortable with higher risk.

A dynamic approach involves adjusting stop-loss and take-profit levels based on changing market conditions. Traders may move stop-loss levels to breakeven once a trade has moved in their favor, or they may trail stop-loss levels behind price movements to lock in profits while allowing for further gains.

In conclusion, setting stop-loss and take-profit levels is crucial to effective risk management and profit maximization in cryptocurrency trading. These levels are automated safeguards, guiding traders to limit potential losses and secure profits.

Balancing risk and reward requires a combination of technical analysis, risk assessment, and understanding of market dynamics. Traders must also consider external factors impacting price movements and adapt their strategies accordingly.

By implementing a well-thought-out approach to setting stop-loss and take-profit levels, traders position themselves to navigate the fast-paced and often unpredictable realm of cryptocurrency trading with confidence, discipline, and the potential for optimized trading outcomes.

Position sizing and determining risk-reward ratios

In the dynamic realm of cryptocurrency trading, where opportunities and risks abound, the principles of position sizing and risk-reward ratios emerge as fundamental pillars of a trader's success. These strategies guide traders in allocating capital wisely, managing risk effectively, and optimizing their trading outcomes. This section explores the nuances of position sizing and determining risk-reward ratios in cryptocurrency trading, delving into the methodologies, considerations, and benefits that shape these essential elements of a trader's toolkit.

Position sizing refers to determining the amount of capital to invest in a single trade. This decision is critical as it directly influences a trade's potential gains and losses. Position sizing goes beyond deciding how much to invest; it's about balancing capital preservation and capital growth.

One common approach to position sizing is the Fixed Percentage Risk Model. In this model, traders decide on a fixed percentage of their trading capital that they are willing to risk on a single trade. For instance, if a trader's risk tolerance is 2% and their trading capital is $10,000, they would allocate $200 as their maximum allowable loss for the trade.

Another approach is the Fixed Dollar Risk Model. Here, traders determine a fixed dollar amount they will risk on each trade. For example, if a trader is comfortable risking $300 per trade, regardless of their account size, they would adjust their position size accordingly.

Market conditions, trade setups, and volatility can also influence position sizing. During periods of high volatility, traders might reduce their position sizes to account for more significant price swings, while during stable market conditions, they might increase their position sizes to capitalize on potential price movements.

The risk-reward ratio is a vital metric that assesses the potential profit of a trade compared to the possible loss. It's a reflection of a trader's willingness to accept risk in pursuit of reward. A favorable risk-reward ratio indicates that the potential reward outweighs the potential loss, making the trade more attractive.

For instance, if a trader is willing to risk $100 on a trade and is targeting a profit of $300, the risk-reward ratio is 1:3. This indicates that if the deal is profitable, the trader stands to make three dollars for every dollar at risk.

A well-balanced risk-reward ratio is pivotal for maintaining a consistent edge in trading. It allows traders to be profitable even if they have a lower success rate, as long as their winning trades deliver more profit than their losing trades incur losses.

Position sizing and risk-reward ratios are essential for a harmonious trading approach.

When determining position sizes, traders should consider their risk tolerance and the amount they are willing to lose on a trade. Traders can calculate the potential profit required to justify the risk using the risk-reward ratio. For example, a trader with a risk tolerance of $200 and a desired risk-reward ratio of 1:2 would aim for a potential profit of $400.

By integrating position sizing and risk-reward ratios, traders align their strategies with their risk appetite and profit goals. This approach helps prevent excessive losses, supports capital growth, and ensures that trades are based on logical and calculated reasoning rather than impulsive decision-making.

Position sizing and risk-reward ratios offer numerous benefits to cryptocurrency traders.

First, they help manage risk. Position sizing ensures that no single trade can lead to a catastrophic loss, preserving capital for future opportunities. The risk-reward ratio balances the potential gains and losses of trades, helping traders maintain a positive expectancy in their trading strategies.

Second, they provide a structured framework for decision-making. By adhering to predetermined position sizes and risk-reward ratios, traders remove emotion from their trading, making rational decisions based on data and analysis.

However, challenges can arise if traders become overconfident or deviate from their position sizing and risk-reward principles. Emotional impulses can lead to larger-than-planned positions or trading setups with unfavorable risk-reward ratios.

Various strategies and variations can be employed based on a trader's risk appetite, trading style, and market conditions.

Aggressive traders might opt for higher risk-reward ratios, seeking higher potential profits while accepting a lower success rate. More conservative traders might prioritize lower risk-reward ratios to increase their likelihood of success.

Pyramiding is a strategy where traders add to their positions as the trade moves in their favor. This approach allows traders to maximize profits while managing risk by adjusting the stop-loss level as the position size increases.

In conclusion, position sizing and determining risk-reward ratios are integral components of a trader's path to profitability in cryptocurrency trading. These strategies guide traders in allocating capital effectively, managing risk prudently, and making informed trading decisions.

By striking a balance between capital preservation and growth, traders position themselves to navigate the volatile and often unpredictable world of cryptocurrencies with confidence and discipline. As a guiding metric, the risk-reward ratio ensures that trades are evaluated not only based on potential gains but also in consideration of potential losses.

As traders venture into the exhilarating arena of cryptocurrency trading, position sizing and risk-reward ratios stand as beacons of calculated decision-making, helping traders seize opportunities, manage risk, and achieve sustainable success in the dynamic and evolving landscape of digital asset trading.

Avoiding overtrading and chasing losses

In the captivating realm of cryptocurrency trading, where excitement and potential profits are juxtaposed with volatility and risk, the pitfalls of overtrading and chasing losses loom large. These tendencies, driven by emotions and impulsivity, can erode capital, undermine strategies, and lead to a cycle of frustration. This section delves into the intricacies of avoiding overtrading and chasing losses in cryptocurrency trading, exploring the methodologies, challenges, and benefits that empower traders to make disciplined decisions and safeguard their trading endeavors.

Overtrading refers to executing a high volume of trades within a short period, often driven by a compulsion to be constantly in the market. While the allure of numerous trading opportunities is tempting, overtrading can result in significant drawbacks.

One of the primary risks of overtrading is increased transaction costs. Frequent trading incurs transaction fees, spreads, and slippage, which can accumulate and eat into profits. Moreover, overtrading often leads to impulsive decisions, as traders act without sufficient analysis and research. This impulsive behavior is more likely to result in losses than carefully considered trades.

Overtrading can also lead to mental and emotional exhaustion. Constantly monitoring the markets, executing trades, and experiencing heightened stress levels can affect a trader's well-being. Decision fatigue and burnout can impair a trader's capacity to make educated decisions and adhere to their plan of action.

Avoiding overtrading requires discipline and patience. Traders should establish a clear trading plan with predefined entry and exit criteria. Each trade should be backed by thorough analysis, rather than impulsive decision-making. By setting specific criteria for trade execution, traders can filter out excessive trades and focus on high-quality setups.

Implementing a trading journal can be immensely helpful. Recording each trade, its rationale, and the outcome provides a tangible record of trading decisions. This enables traders to identify patterns of overtrading and learn from past mistakes.

Another strategy is to set a daily or weekly trading limit. By limiting the number of trades per day or week, traders force themselves to be selective and focus on quality over quantity. Additionally, allocating specific time slots for trading activities helps prevent the constant monitoring of markets that can lead to overtrading.

Chasing losses, often driven by emotions like frustration, anger, or the desire to "get back" at the market, involves increasing the size or frequency of trades to recover losses incurred in previous trades. This impulsive behavior can amplify losses and lead to a downward spiral.

Chasing losses is fraught with risks. Emotional decision-making clouds judgment and often results in hasty and ill-conceived trades. Traders may abandon their strategy, take excessive risks, or enter trades without proper analysis, all desperately attempting to recover losses.

Chasing losses can also lead to a depletion of capital. To recover quickly, traders may use larger position sizes, putting more capital at risk and exacerbating the losses. The emotional toll of chasing losses can create a cycle of negative emotions, further impairing a trader's ability to make rational decisions.

Avoiding the trap of chasing losses requires a commitment to rational decision-making and emotional discipline. Traders must accept that losses are a natural part of trading and that attempting to recover them quickly is counterproductive.

Maintaining a trading journal, as mentioned earlier, plays a pivotal role in preventing the cycle of chasing losses. By documenting losses, traders can objectively review their trades and identify whether the losses were due to poor decision-making or simply part of the normal ebb and flow of trading.

Another strategy is to establish a maximum loss threshold for each trade. Once this threshold is reached, the trader stops trading for the day. This strategy prevents escalating losses and allows one to regroup and analyze what went wrong.

Avoiding overtrading and chasing losses yields significant benefits for cryptocurrency traders.

First, disciplined decision-making preserves capital. By avoiding excessive trades and impulsive decisions, traders protect their capital from unnecessary risk and keep it for high-quality setups.

Second, disciplined traders can maintain a clear and rational mindset. Emotional reactions are minimized, allowing traders to make well-considered decisions based on analysis and strategy.

Third, disciplined traders are better positioned for consistent profitability. By adhering to their trading plans and avoiding emotional revenge trading, traders increase their chances of executing trades that align with their strategies.

In conclusion, avoiding overtrading and chasing losses is essential to prudent and disciplined cryptocurrency trading. These behaviors, driven by emotion and impulsivity, can undermine trading strategies, erode capital, and compromise a trader's mental well-being.

By embracing strategies such as setting predefined criteria for trades, maintaining trading journals, and imposing trading limits, traders empower themselves to make rational decisions based on analysis rather than emotion. This disciplined approach safeguards capital and enhances the likelihood of consistent profitability.

CHAPTER IX

Developing Your Trading Plan

Creating a personalized trading plan

In the fast-paced and exhilarating realm of cryptocurrency trading, creating a personalized trading plan is a guiding light for traders seeking consistent success amidst volatility and uncertainty. A trading plan is not merely a set of rules but a strategic blueprint that aligns a trader's goals, risk tolerance, and methodology into a cohesive framework. This section delves into the nuances of creating a personalized trading plan in cryptocurrency trading, exploring the essential components, considerations, and benefits that empower traders to navigate the complex landscape with confidence and discipline.

A trading plan is the cornerstone of a trader's journey. It provides structure, clarity, and direction in an environment where impulsive decisions and emotional reactions can lead to significant losses. A well-crafted trading plan equips traders with the tools to make informed decisions, manage risk, and stay focused on their goals. The trading plan is a roadmap, helping traders stay grounded amid market fluctuations. It encompasses various aspects of trading, including strategy development, risk management, trade execution, and psychological preparedness.

The trading plan should outline the trading strategy a trader will follow. This includes the approach to technical and fundamental analysis, timeframes, and the types of trades (day trading, swing trading, etc.). Clearly defining risk management guidelines is essential. This involves deciding how much capital to risk on each trade, defining stop-loss and take-profit levels, and setting maximum daily or weekly loss limits. Traders should specify how they will determine the size of each position based on their risk tolerance and account size. This ensures that position sizes are consistent and aligned with the trader's overall risk management strategy.

Detailing how trades will be executed is crucial. This includes the criteria for entering a trade, the types of orders to be used (market orders, limit orders, etc.), and the conditions for trade closure. Outline the types of analysis that will guide trading decisions. This could include technical analysis, fundamental analysis, or a combination of both. Specify the indicators, chart patterns, and other tools that will be utilized. Keeping a trade journal to record each trade, the reasoning behind it, and the outcome is vital. This journal provides a historical record allowing traders to analyze their decisions and learn from successes and failures. Addressing the psychological aspect of trading is essential. Traders should outline managing emotions, staying disciplined, and handling drawdown periods or losses.

A personalized trading plan should reflect the trader's unique circumstances, risk tolerance, and trading style. It's not a one-size-fits-all template but a tailored strategy that resonates with the individual trader. To customize the plan, traders must take an honest inventory of their strengths and weaknesses. This includes acknowledging their risk tolerance, preferred timeframes, technical analysis skills, and market knowledge. By aligning the trading plan with their strengths, traders position themselves for success.

Making a trading plan is a continuous process that involves testing, enhancing and modifying. To test their strategy in a safe environment, traders should begin with a demo account. This allows them to identify potential flaws and areas for improvement without risking real capital. As traders gain experience and gather data from their demo trading, they can refine their plans based on real-world insights. Adjustments might be made to trading strategies, risk management rules, or the types of analysis used.

A personalized trading plan offers several benefits to cryptocurrency traders. First, it provides clarity and structure. Traders know precisely what they need to do in different market scenarios, reducing the uncertainty and emotional decision-making that can lead to losses. Second, it instills discipline. Following a well-defined plan helps traders avoid impulsive and emotionally driven trades. This disciplined approach leads to better risk management and more consistent profitability. Third, it enhances psychological resilience. A plan in place equips traders to handle losses and drawdowns with a balanced perspective. Emotional reactions are minimized, and traders can stay focused on their long-term goals.

In conclusion, creating a personalized trading plan in cryptocurrency trading is a fundamental step toward achieving consistent success in a volatile and dynamic environment. This plan acts as a compass, guiding traders through the challenges and opportunities of the market while mitigating risks and emotional pitfalls. By encompassing goals, trading strategies, risk management, and psychological preparedness, a well-crafted trading plan empowers traders to make informed decisions, stick to their strategies, and achieve sustainable profitability. As traders embark on the exciting journey of cryptocurrency trading, a personalized trading plan stands as a beacon of discipline, resilience, and the potential for long-term success in digital assets.

Setting goals and defining your trading style

The importance of setting goals and deciding on a trading strategy cannot be overstated in the exciting world of cryptocurrency trading, where fortunes can be gained and lost in the span of a single glance. Cryptocurrency markets, characterized by their volatility and potential for substantial gains, require traders to navigate with purpose and strategy. This section delves into the intricate realm of setting trading goals and defining a trading style in cryptocurrency trading, exploring the nuances, considerations, and benefits that guide traders toward effective decision-making and sustainable success.

Setting clear and achievable trading goals is akin to creating a roadmap for success. Without well-defined goals, traders risk drifting aimlessly through the tumultuous waters of the cryptocurrency market, susceptible to emotional impulses and rash decisions. Trading goals serve as a lighthouse, illuminating the path ahead and keeping traders focused on their desired outcomes. Trading goals can encompass a range of objectives, from short-term gains to long-term wealth accumulation. They include achieving a specific percentage return on investment, consistently outperforming a market benchmark, or generating a certain amount of profit over a defined period. These goals act as anchors, grounding traders in their pursuit of profitability and acting as a gauge to measure progress.

Setting effective trading goals requires a structured approach. Traders should begin by evaluating their financial circumstances, risk tolerance, and available time commitment. These factors influence the type of goals that are realistic and achievable. A trader with a full-time job and limited time for trading might have different goals than a full-time professional trader. Additionally, goals should be specific, measurable, achievable, relevant, and time-bound (SMART). A vague goal like "make more money" lacks specificity and is challenging to measure. Instead, a SMART goal might be "achieve a 15% return on investment over the next six months."

Just as a ship requires a skilled captain to navigate rough seas, a trader needs a defined trading style to navigate the complexities of the cryptocurrency market. A trading style encapsulates the trader's approach to analyzing the market, making trading decisions, and managing risk. It reflects the trader's personality, risk tolerance, and market outlook.

Several trading styles exist within the cryptocurrency realm. Day traders make numerous trades in a single day to profit from short-term price changes. This style demands quick decision-making, technical analysis skills, and the ability to manage risk within a limited timeframe. Swing traders hold positions for several days to weeks, aiming to capture medium-term price movements. This approach requires a balance between technical and fundamental analysis. Scalpers seek to make quick profits from minute price changes. This style requires intense focus, discipline, and the ability to manage risk in a fast-paced environment. Position traders take a longer-term perspective, holding positions for weeks, months, or even years. This style often incorporates fundamental analysis and requires patience and a strong conviction in the investment thesis. Trend followers identify and capitalize on sustained price trends. This style requires the ability to identify trends early and the discipline to ride them until they reverse.

Defining a trading style offers several benefits to cryptocurrency traders. First, it aligns trading decisions with the trader's strengths and preferences. A trader who enjoys analyzing short-term price movements is better suited for day trading than long-term investing. Second, a defined trading style guides decision-making. It helps traders identify suitable entry and exit points, set stop-loss levels, and manage risk more effectively. Third, it promotes consistency. A consistent trading style helps traders develop expertise in specific strategies and techniques, improving decision-making over time.

In conclusion, setting goals and defining a trading style form the bedrock of success in cryptocurrency trading. Goals provide direction, motivation, and a benchmark for measuring progress. A well-structured goal-setting process ensures that traders align their aspirations with their circumstances and available resources. Defining a trading style empowers traders to navigate the cryptocurrency market with purpose and strategy. By choosing a style that resonates with their personality, risk tolerance, and strengths, traders position themselves to make informed decisions, manage risk, and achieve sustainable success. As traders embark on the exhilarating journey of cryptocurrency trading, setting goals and defining a trading style serves as a compass, guiding them through the complexities of the market. With clear objectives and a defined approach, traders are better equipped to navigate the highs and lows, capitalize on opportunities, and chart a course toward profitability and long-term success in the dynamic world of digital assets.

Incorporating technical, fundamental, and sentiment analysis

The world of cryptocurrency trading, marked by its rapid pace and high volatility, demands a comprehensive approach to decision-making. Traders navigate a landscape where market trends can shift instantly, and profit opportunities emerge and fade in the blink of an eye. In this intricate ecosystem, the combination of technical, fundamental, and sentiment analysis provides traders with a multi-dimensional toolkit for understanding the market's intricacies, making informed decisions, and capitalizing on opportunities.

At the core of effective cryptocurrency trading lie three key pillars of analysis: technical, fundamental, and sentiment analysis. Each of these pillars offers a distinct perspective on the market dynamics. Technical analysis entails the study of historical price data and the identification of patterns that can guide future price movements. This approach is underpinned by the idea that past price behavior can offer insights into future trends. On the other hand, fundamental analysis delves into the underlying factors that influence an asset's value.

This includes evaluating the project's whitepaper, technology, team, partnerships, adoption rate, and regulatory environment. Lastly, sentiment analysis revolves around gauging the mood of the market. This can be realized by analyzing social media trends, news sentiment, and market sentiment indicators.

While each form of analysis provides valuable insights, the real power emerges when these approaches are integrated. By weaving together technical, fundamental, and sentiment analysis, traders gain a comprehensive and nuanced understanding of the market landscape. This synergistic approach enables traders to discern significant patterns, filter out noise, and make decisions based on a more comprehensive data set.

The integration of these analyses often leads to the convergence of signals. When technical indicators, fundamental analysis, and sentiment indicators align, traders receive stronger and more convincing signals. For instance, a bullish technical pattern supported by positive news sentiment and robust fundamentals creates a compelling case for entering a trade.

Furthermore, the integration of analyses offers enhanced risk mitigation. In cases where technical analysis suggests a specific direction, but fundamental or sentiment analysis provides a contradictory outlook, traders are prompted to reassess their decisions. This layered approach acts as a safety net, preventing traders from falling into traps triggered by reliance on a single analysis type.

While technical analysis often focuses on short-term trends, including fundamental analysis lends a long-term perspective. The marriage of these two approaches enables traders to identify assets with promising long-term potential that simultaneously exhibit favorable short-term technical patterns. This equilibrium between short and long-term viewpoints assists in constructing well-rounded trading strategies.

In cryptocurrency trading, emotions can be both a trader's greatest asset and their Achilles' heel. Here, sentiment analysis plays a vital role by assisting traders in managing emotional biases. During extreme market sentiment, such as FOMO (Fear of Missing Out) or FUD (Fear, Uncertainty, Doubt), sentiment analysis is a compass, guiding traders to stay grounded and make rational decisions.

However, the integration of these analyses has its challenges. Traders must grapple with conflicting signals and discern the reliability of various sources of information. Additionally, the rapid pace at which the cryptocurrency market operates can make it challenging to synthesize data and make timely decisions.

In conclusion, incorporating technical, fundamental, and sentiment analysis in cryptocurrency trading is akin to wielding a triad of wisdom. While each analysis type provides unique insights, their true potency is unveiled when harmoniously integrated. This holistic approach empowers traders to make well-informed decisions by considering historical price patterns, intrinsic value drivers, and prevailing market sentiment. By harnessing the strengths of each analysis type, traders are better equipped to navigate the intricate cryptocurrency market, seize opportunities, and maneuver through its ever-evolving landscape with confidence and precision. As traders aspire to master the art of cryptocurrency trading, the integration of technical, fundamental, and sentiment analysis stands as a beacon of enlightenment, guiding them toward the achievement of consistent success in this dynamic and exhilarating domain.

Testing and adjusting your trading plan over time

In the fast-paced world of cryptocurrency trading, the ability to adapt and evolve is paramount. While a well-crafted trading plan provides a solid foundation, the dynamic nature of the market demands continuous testing, assessment, and adjustment. This section delves into the significance of testing and adjusting a trading plan over time in cryptocurrency trading, exploring the iterative process, the benefits of adaptability, and how traders can navigate the complexities of market evolution while pursuing consistent success.

Cryptocurrency markets are characterized by their volatility, innovation, and ever-changing dynamics. What worked as a winning strategy yesterday may prove ineffective or risky tomorrow. Thus, the notion of evolving one's trading plan over time is not a luxury but a necessity. Traders who fail to adapt risk being left behind as the market transforms around them.

Testing and adjusting a trading plan is an iterative process, much like refining a work of art. Traders begin by implementing their initial plan and observing its performance in real-world trading scenarios. The outcomes of these trades serve as valuable data points that inform decision-making. If certain aspects of the plan yield consistent success, traders can reinforce those strategies. Conversely, if certain elements consistently lead to losses or suboptimal outcomes, it's a cue for adjustment.

Effective testing and adjustment are rooted in data-driven decision-making. Traders must meticulously record their trades, outcomes, and the rationale behind each decision. Over time, patterns emerge, revealing strengths and weaknesses in the trading plan. By analyzing this data, traders can make informed adjustments that are aligned with their trading goals.

The benefits of testing and adjusting a trading plan are manifold. Firstly, it enhances adaptability. Traders who evolve their strategies based on real-world performance are better positioned to seize new opportunities and mitigate emerging risks. Secondly, it improves decision-making. By relying on empirical data, traders make decisions grounded in evidence rather than emotion or intuition. Thirdly, it hones skills. The iterative testing and adjustment process refines traders' analytical and strategic skills, promoting continuous improvement.

The testing and adjustment process involves fine-tuning various trading plan elements. This includes tweaking entry and exit strategies, modifying risk management parameters, and incorporating new indicators or analysis techniques. Traders might also reassess the alignment of their trading style with market conditions, adjusting their approach accordingly.

Many factors, including technological advancements, regulatory changes, and shifts in investor sentiment, influence cryptocurrency markets. A trading plan that thrived in a bull market may struggle in a bear market and vice versa. Traders must adapt their strategies to account for changing market conditions. This might involve shifting from aggressive day trading to more conservative swing trading during periods of uncertainty.

While testing and adjusting a trading plan is crucial, it has challenges. Emotional attachment to a certain strategy or the reluctance to abandon a once-successful approach can hinder the adjustment process. Additionally, overreacting to short-term losses or prematurely changing strategies due to a lack of patience can lead to suboptimal outcomes.

Successful testing and adjustment require a combination of patience and consistency. Traders must avoid making impulsive changes based on isolated events. Instead, they should assess data over a significant period to identify trends and patterns that warrant adjustments. Consistency in recording and analyzing trades ensures a robust foundation for decision-making.

In conclusion, testing and adjusting a trading plan over time is essential in cryptocurrency trading. The dynamic nature of the market demands adaptability and continuous improvement. Traders who commit to this iterative process benefit from data-driven decision-making, improved strategies, and the ability to navigate changing market conditions with finesse. Through meticulous data collection, analysis, and the courage to embrace change, traders pave the way for sustainable success in the volatile and exhilarating world of cryptocurrency trading. As the market continues to evolve, the practice of testing and adjusting remains a steadfast ally in the pursuit of consistency and excellence.

CHAPTER X

Case Studies and Real-World Examples

Analyzing successful and unsuccessful trades

Trading cryptocurrencies is a high-risk activity where fortunes may be gained or lost in a matter of seconds. Analyzing successful and unsuccessful trades holds profound value in this volatile landscape. Such analysis is not merely a retrospective exercise; it is a window into the trader's decision-making process, a treasure trove of insights, and a catalyst for growth. This section delves into the importance of dissecting trades, the lessons gleaned from both victories and setbacks, and how traders can leverage this introspection to refine their strategies, minimize mistakes, and nurture a path toward long-term success.

A successful trade is not just a profit; it's an opportunity to learn. By dissecting the elements that contributed to success, traders can unearth the specific strategies, indicators, or market conditions that played a pivotal role. This introspection transforms success into education, allowing traders to replicate winning strategies in future trades.

Traders must scrutinize the outcomes and the underlying factors that fueled success. Was it a well-timed entry based on technical analysis? Did fundamental research reveal a hidden gem? Did a contrarian strategy pay off due to prevailing market sentiment? By identifying the driving forces, traders can create a playbook of proven effective strategies under specific circumstances.

While analyzing successful trades is beneficial, traders must guard against overconfidence. Success can sometimes be attributed to market luck rather than sound decision-making. By critically examining the factors at play, traders remain grounded, ensuring that successes are built on a foundation of consistent strategy rather than luck.

Unsuccessful trades are often regarded as failures, but they hold unparalleled lessons. When a trade goes awry, it's an opportunity to examine missteps and avoid repeating them. Instead of viewing losses as defeats, traders can reframe them as tuition fees for valuable market education.

By delving into unsuccessful trades, traders can pinpoint errors and misjudgments that led to losses. Did impulsive decision-making override technical analysis? Were emotions at the helm of a trade? Did the trade violate risk management rules? Identifying these pitfalls helps traders become more disciplined and less susceptible to repeating past mistakes.

Risk management often plays a pivotal role in unsuccessful trades. By assessing whether trades adhered to predetermined risk parameters, traders can gauge the effectiveness of their risk management strategies. Did a trade's stop-loss level provide adequate protection? Was the position size appropriate for the risk tolerance? These insights refine risk management practices and mitigate potential future losses.

Journaling trades is a powerful practice that provides clarity and accountability. Traders who meticulously document their thought processes, analysis, and emotions leading up to each trade gain a comprehensive record of their trading journey. This journal becomes a treasure trove for analyzing both successful and unsuccessful trades, facilitating self-awareness and growth.

The iterative process of analyzing trades and adjusting strategies is a hallmark of successful trading. Traders who recognize the evolving nature of the market and the need for continuous improvement are better equipped to adapt to changing conditions. Analyzing trades facilitates the refinement of strategies over time, ensuring that traders remain nimble and effective in navigating the dynamic cryptocurrency landscape.

The act of analyzing trades serves as a buffer against emotional decision-making. Emotions like fear and greed can cloud judgment and lead to irrational decisions. By objectively examining trades, traders can extract insights based on data rather than emotions, enabling more rational and disciplined decision-making in the future.

In conclusion, analyzing both successful and unsuccessful trades is not just a retrospective exercise; it's a journey of growth and mastery in cryptocurrency trading. By dissecting the factors that led to success and setbacks, traders refine their strategies, fine-tune their decision-making processes, and cultivate resilience. Each trade becomes a stepping stone toward greater self-awareness and expertise, enabling traders to navigate the volatility and complexities of the cryptocurrency market with wisdom and finesse. The practice of trade analysis transforms the trading journey from a series of transactions into a meaningful quest for improvement, empowering traders to build a foundation of consistency and long-term success in this ever-evolving arena.

Learning from past market trends and events

With its inherent volatility and rapid shifts, cryptocurrency trading is a realm where learning from the past is as invaluable as predicting the future. Historical market trends and events serve as a treasure trove of insights in this ever-changing landscape. By delving into the annals of cryptocurrency history, traders can glean invaluable lessons, identify recurring patterns, and make informed decisions that transcend transient market sentiments. This section delves into the significance of learning from past market trends and events in cryptocurrency trading, exploring the benefits of historical analysis, the wisdom hidden within trends, and how traders can utilize this knowledge to navigate the complexities of the digital asset realm with prudence and confidence.

Dramatic shifts, exponential growth, and unexpected turns mark the history of cryptocurrency markets. From the meteoric rise of Bitcoin to the proliferation of altcoins, and from the ICO boom to regulatory crackdowns, the cryptocurrency landscape has witnessed many trends and events that have shaped its trajectory. These events serve as case studies in the interplay of market forces, investor psychology, and technological innovation.

Much like traditional financial markets, cryptocurrency markets exhibit patterns that repeat over time. By examining historical price charts and correlating them with significant events, traders can identify recurring patterns that offer predictive value. Whether it's a pattern of price spikes preceding major conferences or a cyclical ebb and flow in market sentiment, these insights equip traders with the ability to anticipate trends and make informed decisions.

Cryptocurrency trends provide a window into the market's collective psyche. The exponential growth of Bitcoin in its early days, the sudden altcoin surge during bull markets, and the periodic downturns all reveal the intricate dance between investor sentiment and market fundamentals. Studying these trends can offer insights into investor behavior, risk appetite, and market maturity.

The wisdom derived from historical analysis can be a guiding light in decision-making. Traders who understand how past events have influenced market trends are better equipped to interpret the present and anticipate the future. For instance, the correlation between regulatory news and price movements can inform trading strategies during periods of potential regulatory announcements.

Major events, whether technological advancements or regulatory shifts, leave an indelible mark on cryptocurrency markets. The success of Ethereum's smart contracts or the market turbulence following China's crypto bans exemplify the significance of such events. Traders who comprehend the impact of these events can position themselves to capitalize on opportunities or safeguard against potential pitfalls.

Learning from past market trends includes understanding the role of sentiment and media. The power of social media, news cycles, and influencer opinions cannot be underestimated. Historical analysis reveals how these factors have catalyzed price movements, triggered FOMO (Fear of Missing Out), or sparked market-wide panic.

History serves as a teacher, not just in the successes but in past mistakes. The market's past is riddled with instances of excessive speculation, pump-and-dump schemes, and overleveraging. By studying past failures, traders can avoid falling into similar traps and make decisions rooted in prudence rather than blind optimism.

Historical analysis provides a semblance of structure in the uncertain world of cryptocurrency trading. While past trends may not guarantee future outcomes, they offer insights into how markets have reacted to similar circumstances in the past. This knowledge empowers traders to approach uncertain situations with more confidence, guided by history lessons.

While historical analysis provides predictive insights, balancing this with adaptability is essential. Cryptocurrency markets are evolving, and new technologies, regulations, and market dynamics can alter established patterns. Traders must remain open to adjusting their strategies based on emerging trends and changing market conditions.

In conclusion, learning from past market trends and events in cryptocurrency trading is akin to wielding an atlas of insights. The market's history is replete with lessons, patterns, and invaluable knowledge waiting to be uncovered. By analyzing trends, identifying recurring patterns, and understanding the influence of historical events, traders can make informed decisions that transcend fleeting market sentiments. This depth of understanding empowers traders to navigate the multifaceted world of cryptocurrency with prudence, anticipation, and confidence. The practice of learning from the past not only enriches the trading journey but also shapes the trajectory toward sustained success in the ever-evolving landscape of digital assets. As traders embark on their quest, the wisdom hidden within historical analysis serves as their guidepost, illuminating the path to informed decision-making in the dynamic realm of cryptocurrency trading.

Exploring different strategies in action

Cryptocurrency trading boasts a spectrum of strategies, each embodying distinct characteristics and catering to various trader preferences. Day trading is at one end of the spectrum, a strategy characterized by its high-frequency nature. Day traders make numerous trades in a single day to profit from short-term price changes. This approach demands quick decision-making, a keen understanding of technical analysis, and an ability to gauge market psychology on a minute-by-minute basis.

Swing trading occupies a middle ground between day trading and long-term investing. Swing traders aim to capture short- to medium-term trends, entering positions as a trend forms and exiting before it reverses. This strategy necessitates a grasp of technical indicators, chart patterns, and market sentiment. Swing traders analyze price charts to identify potential entry and exit points, with holding periods ranging from a few days to several weeks.

On the opposite end of the spectrum lies long-term investing, a strategy synonymous with patience and a macro perspective. Long-term investors buy and hold assets for extended periods, relying on fundamental analysis to assess a project's viability, technology, and potential for adoption. This approach requires conviction in the long-term growth potential of a cryptocurrency and an ability to withstand market volatility without being swayed by short-term fluctuations.

Scalping, another strategy in the trader's toolkit, involves capturing small price movements through rapid trades. Scalpers execute numerous trades within a short timeframe, relying on technical analysis and tight stop- loss and take-profit orders to secure minimal gains from each trade. This strategy demands precision, discipline, and an understanding of transaction costs, as frequent trades can accumulate fees.

Momentum trading follows the herds of market sentiment, aiming to capitalize on strong price movements catalyzed by news, events, or sentiment shifts. Traders who employ this strategy seek to enter positions as trends gain momentum and exit before the momentum wanes. Momentum traders utilize both technical and sentiment analysis to identify optimal entry and exit points, harnessing the power of market psychology to their advantage.

Buying an asset on one exchange where the price is cheaper and selling it on a different one where the price is higher is known as arbitrage, a method that takes advantage of price differences. Traders who specialize in arbitrage rely on swift execution and continuous monitoring of price differences across various platforms. This strategy requires vigilance, quick decision-making, and understanding exchange dynamics.

Factors influencing the selection of a trading strategy include individual risk tolerance, availability of time, prevailing market conditions, and the trader's skill set. Traders with a higher risk tolerance may gravitate towards day trading or scalping, while those seeking stable returns may lean towards swing trading or long-term investing. Time availability is also pivotal; day trading and scalping demand constant market monitoring, while swing trading and long-term investing offer a more relaxed pace.

Market conditions are critical in strategy selection, as different approaches thrive under varying circumstances. Traders must align their chosen strategy with the prevailing market sentiment and trend direction. The ability to accurately assess market conditions allows traders to deploy strategies best suited to capitalize on emerging opportunities or safeguard against potential risks.

Market analysis skills are paramount in executing various strategies effectively. Traders relying on day trading, scalping, and swing trading must possess adept technical analysis capabilities to identify trends, patterns, and probable entry and exit points. In contrast, long-term investors prioritize fundamental analysis, evaluating a cryptocurrency project's technology, use case, and adoption potential.

Real-world examples illuminate the application of different strategies. A day trader might spot an uptrend in Bitcoin's price following positive news, promptly enter a long position, and exit for profit before the trend reverses. A swing trader might leverage an Ethereum price pattern of higher lows and higher highs, entering during a pullback and exiting before the trend loses momentum. A long-term investor might thoroughly research an altcoin project's fundamentals, invest with a long-term perspective, and ride out market fluctuations.

In conclusion, exploring different strategies in cryptocurrency trading is akin to navigating a landscape of diversity. Each strategy offers a unique approach to the market, catering to different risk tolerances, time availabilities, and market conditions. The spectrum ranges from high-frequency day trading to patient long-term investing, with swing trading, scalping, momentum trading, and arbitrage filling the gaps in between. Success in cryptocurrency trading hinges on selecting a strategy aligned with personal preferences and risk appetite, while adapting to the fluidity of market conditions. The pursuit of trading excellence requires a deep understanding of each strategy and the wisdom to apply them in the right context, ensuring that traders navigate the dynamic cryptocurrency landscape with skill, adaptability, and success.

Lessons and takeaways from the case studies

In the ever-evolving world of cryptocurrency trading, lessons gleaned from real-world case studies serve as beacons of knowledge, illuminating the path to informed decision-making. These case studies offer a vivid tapestry of experiences, successes, failures, and insights that traders can draw upon to navigate the complexities of the digital asset landscape. This section delves into the importance of studying case studies in cryptocurrency trading, the valuable lessons they offer, and how traders can leverage this knowledge to refine their strategies, mitigate risks, and foster a journey of continuous improvement.

Case studies bridge theory and practice, allowing traders to witness strategies, decisions, and outcomes in action. The unique blend of context, analysis, and results in case studies offers a holistic view of trading dynamics that textbooks or theoretical concepts alone cannot provide.

Case studies encapsulate both success stories and failures, making them an invaluable resource for traders. By deconstructing the elements that contributed to triumphs and setbacks, traders gain insights into the factors that drove success or led to failure. This introspection empowers traders to replicate successful strategies and avoid pitfalls that others have encountered.

Case studies offer a front-row seat to the intricate dance of market dynamics. Traders can observe how price movements correlate with news, regulatory developments, partnerships, and technological advancements. This understanding enables traders to make more informed decisions, capitalizing on market trends and anticipating potential shifts.

Case studies provide a canvas for exploring risk management strategies. Analyzing how traders navigated risks and managed positions can inspire others to fine-tune their own risk mitigation techniques. Additionally, case studies highlight the importance of adapting strategies based on market conditions and signals.

Emotions play a pivotal role in trading outcomes; case studies vividly demonstrate this aspect. By examining how emotions influence decision-making in various scenarios, traders can learn to recognize and manage emotional biases that can lead to impulsive actions.

Case studies underscore the dangers of overconfidence and FOMO (Fear of Missing Out). Traders who experienced significant losses due to overestimating their abilities or chasing after market trends offer cautionary tales. By analyzing such instances, traders can cultivate humility and temper their decisions with prudence. Historical market events, such as the Bitcoin halving or regulatory announcements, provide invaluable insights. Case studies highlighting how these events influenced price trends, market sentiment, and investor behavior offer a blueprint for navigating similar occurrences in the future.

Successful trading requires adaptability, and case studies exemplify this trait. Traders who modified their strategies based on changing market conditions, technological shifts, or regulatory changes often emerged stronger. Analyzing such adaptability showcases the importance of remaining agile in a dynamic market landscape.

The Bitcoin bull run of 2017 serves as a quintessential case study. Traders witnessed unprecedented price surges, FOMO-driven buying, and an influx of new market participants. However, the euphoria was followed by a prolonged bear market. This case study underscores the significance of risk management, resisting emotional impulses, and having a clear exit strategy during extreme market volatility.

The case of Ripple (XRP) provides a valuable lesson in the influence of regulatory news on cryptocurrency prices. When regulatory agencies targeted XRP due to concerns about its status as a security, the price plummeted. This case study underscores the importance of staying informed about regulatory developments and their potential consequences for specific cryptocurrencies.

The decentralized finance (DeFi) boom witnessed a surge in token prices and a flurry of new projects. However, the subsequent bust exposed vulnerabilities, rug pulls, and unsustainable projects. This case study highlights the need for due diligence, discerning between solid projects and speculative ones, and maintaining a cautious approach in the face of market exuberance.

In conclusion, case studies in cryptocurrency trading offer a wealth of lessons and takeaways that enrich traders' understanding and decision-making capabilities. These real-world narratives encapsulate successes, failures, market dynamics, emotional factors, and adaptation strategies. By dissecting case studies, traders gain insights into the multifaceted nature of trading, empowering them to make informed decisions, refine their strategies, and cultivate a continuous improvement mindset. The stories of triumphs and tribulations become a crucible of experience from which traders draw wisdom, resilience, and the capacity to thrive in a landscape where knowledge is not just power—it's the key to unlocking the potential of successful cryptocurrency trading.

CONCLUSION

Recap of key points covered in the book

As we journey through the diverse and intricate landscape of cryptocurrency trading, we must reflect on the key points and insights that this book has illuminated. From understanding the fundamentals of cryptocurrencies to exploring various trading strategies and delving into risk management and market analysis, this recap encapsulates the wealth of knowledge gained throughout this book.

At the outset, we embarked on a journey into the world of cryptocurrencies, unraveling the very essence of these digital assets. We explored the concept of blockchain technology—the underpinning of cryptocurrencies— grasping its decentralized nature and potential to revolutionize industries beyond finance.

Diving deeper, we explored the landscape of cryptocurrencies, encountering a vast array of coins and tokens, each with distinct use cases and functionalities. From Bitcoin's role as a pioneer to the innovative features of altcoins like Ethereum, we understood how cryptocurrencies go beyond mere digital money, transforming industries through smart contracts, decentralized applications, and more.

Our journey into cryptocurrency trading commenced with the basics—buy, sell, and hold. We discovered that trading isn't merely about making transactions but is also a skillful practice that requires careful analysis, patience, and a deep understanding of market trends.

Understanding different order types—market, limit, and stop orders—was crucial in mastering the art of trading. We also delved into risk management strategies, recognizing their pivotal role in preserving capital and mitigating losses.

The psychology of trading proved to be a cornerstone of success. We explored how managing emotions, overcoming biases, and cultivating a disciplined mindset are essential for consistent trading success.

As we explored key indicators, chart patterns, and trend analysis, technical analysis became our compass for navigating the markets. This tool unveiled trends, provided insights, and equipped us to make informed trading decisions.

Recognizing that price charts tell only part of the story, we embraced fundamental analysis to delve into the heart of cryptocurrencies. We dissected factors like adoption, partnerships, regulation, and technological advancements, understanding their influence on market sentiment and prices.

Our exploration extended to market sentiment, where we uncovered the role of sentiment in driving market trends. We also delved into sentiment analysis tools and methods, tapping into the power of data and public sentiment.

The fusion of technical, fundamental, and sentiment analysis emerged as a comprehensive strategy for interpreting the complex cryptocurrency landscape. We realized that adopting a multifaceted approach equips us with a holistic perspective, enabling better decision-making.

Real-world case studies illuminated our path, showcasing traders' triumphs, challenges, and insights. From the Bitcoin bull run of 2017 to the DeFi boom and bust, these stories provided tangible lessons in strategy, risk management, and emotional resilience.

Our journey culminated in creating personalized trading plans, tailored to individual goals, risk tolerance, and strategies. These plans serve as roadmaps, guiding traders through the complexities of the market with clarity and confidence.

In this book, we embarked on a journey of knowledge and growth in cryptocurrency trading. From mastering technical and fundamental analysis to understanding market sentiment and crafting trading plans, we've traversed a landscape teeming with insights and opportunities. Remember, success in cryptocurrency trading isn't guaranteed, but by arming ourselves with knowledge, discipline, and adaptability, we enhance our prospects of making informed decisions, navigating market trends, and embracing the evolving nature of the digital asset universe. As you forge ahead on your trading journey, may the lessons learned within these pages serve as your compass, guiding you with wisdom and empowering you to thrive in the dynamic world of cryptocurrency trading.

Emphasizing the ongoing learning process in cryptocurrency trading

Cryptocurrency trading is a testament to the necessity of perpetual learning in a rapidly changing environment. The realm of digital assets is characterized by its dynamic nature—technological advancements, regulatory shifts, and market trends evolve at an astonishing pace.

Consequently, embracing an ongoing learning process cannot be overstated.

Survival in cryptocurrency trading hinges on adaptability—a trait cultivated through continuous learning. As species evolve to thrive in changing environments, traders must develop their strategies, approaches, and mindsets to stay competitive. An individual content with static knowledge risks becoming obsolete, missing out on emerging trends and opportunities.

Technological advancements drive the blockchain ecosystem, the foundation of cryptocurrencies. New consensus mechanisms, scalability solutions, and privacy features emerge, altering the dynamics of digital assets.

Staying informed about these changes is pivotal to assessing their potential impact on prices, adoption, and market sentiment. Without a commitment to ongoing learning, traders risk basing decisions on outdated information, compromising their effectiveness in an ever-evolving market.

Regulatory changes further underscore the need for perpetual learning. Governments worldwide grapple with the task of regulating cryptocurrencies, resulting in shifts that significantly influence the market. Traders who stay informed about regulatory developments can position themselves to navigate potential disruptions and anticipate how legal changes might impact the value and trading of specific cryptocurrencies.

Educational resources abound in the digital age, providing traders with unprecedented access to knowledge. Online courses, webinars, blogs, podcasts, and forums offer insights, technical analysis, and expert perspectives. Engaging with these resources empowers traders to learn from industry veterans, broaden their understanding, and gain new perspectives on trading strategies.

The act of learning extends beyond formal education to the introspection of past trades—both successes and failures. Traders can dissect their decisions, identify patterns, and understand what contributed to their outcomes. This process not only refines strategies but also builds a repository of experiences that guide future decisions, enhancing adaptability and resilience.

A curious mindset catalyzes perpetual learning. Embracing curiosity compels traders to explore new cryptocurrencies, delve into whitepapers, understand technical intricacies, and ask probing questions. This approach enhances traders' competitive edge by enabling them to navigate the complexities of the market with depth and insight.

Community engagement within the cryptocurrency sphere contributes to the ongoing learning process. Platforms like Reddit, Twitter, and Discord host discussions on market trends, projects, and news. Active participation in these conversations fosters collaboration, idea-sharing, and the exchange of diverse perspectives.

Ultimately, the cryptocurrency market's volatility underscores its unpredictability, reinforcing the need for ongoing learning. This commitment to education instills humility by acknowledging that even seasoned traders do not possess all the answers. It encourages a mindset of caution, curiosity, and a willingness to adapt, all of which are essential attributes in a landscape characterized by rapid change.

In conclusion, cryptocurrency trading is a journey of evolution, transformation, and continuous learning. As the landscape shifts, strategies evolve, and market dynamics change, pursuing knowledge becomes the basis for trading success. By embracing ongoing learning, traders position themselves to capitalize on technological advancements, navigate regulatory shifts, and adapt to unforeseen challenges. The journey of perpetual learning shapes traders into astute, adaptable, and resilient navigators of the ever-evolving cryptocurrency trading landscape.

Encouragement to continue improving trading skills and staying updated

In cryptocurrency trading, the pursuit of excellence is an ongoing journey that demands perpetual learning and a commitment to staying updated. As traders navigate this dynamic landscape's complexities, refining trading skills and embracing continuous improvement becomes paramount.

Cryptocurrency trading isn't a static endeavor—it's a journey of evolution. What worked yesterday might not suffice today due to emerging technologies, evolving market trends, and shifting regulations. Recognizing this reality is the first step towards nurturing a mindset that values growth and adaptability.

The quest for trading mastery is a continuous endeavor. Beyond the initial stages of learning, successful traders persistently refine their strategies, enhance technical analysis skills, and explore novel approaches that align with the ever-changing market conditions. This process requires dedication, discipline, and an unwavering commitment to excellence.

In this rapidly advancing landscape, technological innovations play a pivotal role. Staying updated on developments such as decentralized finance (DeFi), non-fungible tokens (NFTs), and blockchain integration in various sectors is essential. By understanding how these technologies influence the market, traders position themselves to seize opportunities and make informed decisions.

A learning mindset is at the core of sustained improvement. Engaging with educational resources, attending webinars, and participating in trading communities fosters an environment conducive to growth. Traders who embrace continuous learning view challenges as stepping stones to progress, leveraging experiences to refine their skills and expand their knowledge.

Resilience is a hallmark of accomplished traders. In a landscape marked by volatility and uncertainty, setbacks are not roadblocks but opportunities for learning. Cultivating resilience empowers traders to adapt to adverse conditions, extract lessons from failures, and emerge stronger, armed with insights contributing to ongoing improvement.

Mistakes are invaluable to teachers on the path to excellence. Traders who approach their errors with humility and a hunger for learning can pinpoint areas that need refinement. Each misstep becomes a blueprint for optimizing risk management strategies, enhancing decision-making processes, and honing trading techniques.

A growth-oriented mindset propels traders towards exceptionalism. Embracing challenges, pushing boundaries, and seeing each trade as an opportunity to learn fuels this mindset. Such an approach accelerates the journey towards becoming a master trader, where continuous growth is not a destination but a way of life.

Staying informed in the ever-changing cryptocurrency landscape requires vigilance. Regulations, technological advancements, and market sentiment can transform rapidly. Traders who prioritize staying updated remain well-prepared to navigate uncertainties, make informed choices, and capitalize on opportunities arising from shifting circumstances.

Mentorship and collaboration are potent catalysts for growth. Learning from experienced traders and mentors provides insights, guidance, and wisdom. Engaging with peers within trading communities fosters collective growth, underscoring the idea that the pursuit of excellence is a collaborative endeavor.

Ultimately, the journey toward improving trading skills and staying updated is a journey of self-discovery. Traders uncover their strengths, identify weaknesses, and map out a growth trajectory. This voyage is a testament to the unbounded potential within every trader, waiting to be unlocked through unwavering dedication.

In conclusion, pursuing excellence in cryptocurrency trading necessitates an unending commitment to growth and knowledge acquisition. As traders, we can continually learn, adapt, and thrive in a dynamic landscape. By embracing continuous improvement, we equip ourselves with the tools to navigate shifting market conditions, seize opportunities, and excel as informed and accomplished traders. This journey is a testament to our potential for greatness—a journey that, when embraced wholeheartedly, elevates our trading skills and enriches our lives.

www.ingramcontent.com/pod-product-compliance
Lightning Source LLC
Chambersburg PA
CBHW050530160726
48003CB00002B/530